The Sober Boozers Club: How to Drink Beer (And Stay Sober)

BEN GIBBS

The Sober Boozers Club: How To Drink Beer (And Stay Sober)

Copyright © 2025 Ben Gibbs

All rights reserved

ISBN: 9798287376437

DEDICATION

For the alcoholic I was—and the beer lover I still am.

The Sober Boozers Club: How To Drink Beer (And Stay Sober)

CONTENTS

	Prologue	1
1	A Brief History Of Alcohol-Free Beer	Pg 9
2	How Alcohol-Free Beer Is Made	Pg 15
3	Common Misconceptions About Alcohol-Free Beer	Pg 31
4	My First Three Years Of Sobriety	Pg 39
5	The Social And Psychological Side Of Alcohol-Free Beer	Pg 46
6	How To Enjoy Alcohol-Free Beer	Pg 58
7	The Many Many Many Many Alcohol-Free Beers I Have Tried	Pg 64
8	The Future Of Alcohol-Free Beer	Pg 115
	Conclusion	Pg 123

ACKNOWLEDGMENTS

To the brewers, makers and dreamers pushing the boundaries of what alcohol-free beer can be: Keep going, we're all rooting for you.

To my friends, family, partner and the Sober Boozers Club community—you've kept me grounded, cheered me on and drunk a fair few beers with me along the way.

And to anyone picking this book up who's wondering if they can live without alcohol—I promise you can, and there's a darn good beer waiting for you when you do.

Cheers to all of you.

-Ben

PROLOGUE

For reasons I've since forgotten, I found myself in the garden of family members I tend to only see once every ten years. I have a feeling it must have been a birthday party; there was food, drinks, and people who seemed shocked when I told them I had driven. This was, of course, an intentional move. It was the height of summer, and I had far better things to be getting on with. The act of driving somewhere seems to make leaving early more viable. I could show my face, have a beer, sail off into the sunset. I laid the groundwork for my early exit as soon as I arrived and did my best to appear sincere when I said I was sorry that it would only be a flying visit. "You can't even have a drink if you've driven then, that's a shame" seemed to be the main concern people had, until a voice called from the kitchen; "Would you like to try an alcohol-free beer?"

Let's get something out of the way right now; if you had told me all those years ago that I would be writing an entire book about alcohol-free beer, I would have laughed and changed the subject. Because let's face it, for years (and rightly so), alcohol-free beer had a reputation of being about as exciting as lukewarm sparkling water, only lukewarm sparkling water was probably more exciting.

I don't know if you remember your first alcohol-free beer. If you do, chances are it was foul. Fortunately, I'm young enough to have missed the days of Kaliber, though my dad has told me how it would leave you with a worse hangover than full-alcohol beer. For me, my indoctrination into the world of alcohol-free beer came in the form of Becks Blue. I'll admit I was dismissive of the concept from the start. I couldn't really understand why somebody would have an alcohol-free beer in their fridge to begin with. However, when the bottle was placed in my hand, I couldn't help but feel a strange mix of curiosity and apprehension. The curiosity of how the drink would taste and the apprehension of what it represented.

I took my first sip and knew in that moment that every doubt in my head was correct. Alcohol-free beer was just as terrible as it sounded. It was flat, sweet, and synthetic. I forced the majority of the liquid down my throat, refused a second one, and said my goodbyes. I didn't think about alcohol-free beer again for a few years. I knew for certain, however, that I would never willingly drink the stuff again. After all, alcohol-free beer was clearly something you would only drink when you absolutely had to, not because you want to.

But here I am, albeit a little older and slower, stone cold sober, singing the praises of the liquid that saved my life. That's a pretty large statement, I realise, but without alcohol-free beer, I wouldn't be here today, and the thing is, I'm not alone. Alcohol-free beer is having a moment. You've got craft breweries dedicating entire lines to it, major brands throwing serious money into making it taste good, and people actually *are* drinking this stuff because they want to, rather than have to.

So what happened? How did alcohol-free beer go from an afterthought to a legitimate choice, and more importantly, why should you give it a shot?

My First Steps

Now, I didn't wake up one morning and realise alcohol-free beer had been missing from my life for all of these years. No, I started drinking alcohol-free beer because I did indeed have to. My relationship with alcohol wasn't one that lasted a particularly long time. I didn't start drinking until my mid-twenties, and I stopped drinking before I turned thirty. However, whilst I was relying on alcohol, it was incredibly dangerous for myself and for the people around me. I first noticed that I was leaning a little more heavily towards alcohol when I started working late shifts. I was using it to get to sleep and to feel I was living a normal life. At the same time, I went through a rather traumatic break-up. This opened the floodgates. Before too long, I was drinking most days, often alone at night.

I had spent most of my adult life on stage as a musician. During this period of turbulence in my own personal life, I saw music as an escape and fully embraced the life of a struggling musician. You name it, I did it. It felt like a healthy release, one that I thought I had probably needed for years. I felt like I was finally becoming the person I always knew I could be. Alcohol to me at this time wasn't so much an issue; it was a social lubricant. I felt like the days of lonely drinking were behind me. I had transformed from a lonely, depressed drinker to a social butterfly. The future for Ben Gibbs was looking bright. Enter, lockdown.

I think we all developed some sort of a relationship with alcohol during lockdown. It became acceptable to open a can at 12 midday. The weather was great, I was lucky enough to have a garden, and for the first time in a long time, I felt like I could spend some time really focusing on myself. As it turns out, this was the worst thing that could possibly happen to a borderline alcoholic with years of unaddressed emotional baggage. I was furious with the world; I refused to see how anything that had happened to me in my past could be my fault. By the end of lockdown, I was back to drinking every day. I had also discovered some very high ABV beers that I absolutely loved.

To most of my friends, when the world opened up again, my personality shift came as quite a shock. For the first time in my life, when I drank, I became nasty. I would lash out at friends and family, I would find excuses to go for a drink, and before long, I would take myself to places where I could drink alone. This all climaxed at a big social event, where my entire social circle happened to be present. This evening, I performed the routine that had become expected of me, only this time I doubled down. I woke the next morning (well, afternoon) and knew that if I didn't give up alcohol before too long, I would have nothing left.

That is, of course, a very condensed narrative. If you want to know my full sobriety story, I have been very open about that all over the internet. But this isn't a book about Ben Gibbs getting sober; this is a book about alcohol-free beer. The two do, however, go hand in hand. There is something about the 'foreverness' of sobriety that is incredibly daunting. If you are a beer fan, imagining a world without it is rather revolting. I assumed sobriety would be about giving up—about abstaining and sacrificing. Beer, after all, was so much more than a tasty beverage; it was a social glue, a ritual, a way to mark the end of a long day or to see in the weekend. It was, in many ways, an unquestioned part of adulthood. Without beer, I felt like it would be impossible to enjoy social events. People would surely treat me differently. I would become an outsider in the places I felt I had always belonged.

Things had changed since my bottle of Becks Blue all those years ago. I had heard of exclusively alcohol-free breweries that had popped up and had been shocked to see how much effort Heineken had put into their alcohol-free beer when I went on the brewery tour in Amsterdam in 2018. With this in mind, I decided to once again dip my toe into the world of alcohol-free beer, though I admit my expectations were low. I ordered a mixed case of various beers from breweries such as Mash Gang, Sheep in Wolf's Clothing, Lervig, and Low Tide (now known as Below Brew Co).

The first beer I drank from said box was a beer called Lager Day Saints, from Sheep in Wolf's Clothing. As you may have gathered, it's a lager. However, this was just about as far removed from the Becks Blues of the world as you can possibly get. It was, well, a lager. Not a replica of a lager, or something close to a lager. I made my way through the first box, followed by another, then another. I also began frequenting the low and no aisles of supermarkets, trying as many beers as possible, from the terrible (and trust me, some of them are still terrible) to the sublime.

I realised just how much had changed in the world of alcohol-free beer. Breweries were experimenting with styles, new flavours and brewing techniques. There were crisp lagers, citrusy IPAs, velvety stouts, herbal wheat beers, tangy sours— each crafted with the same passion and dedication as their alcoholic counterparts.

What started as a curiosity and tool to help me navigate the early days of sobriety turned into something much bigger. I began to see alcohol-free beer as more than a drink; it was a vehicle of change, a sign of an evolving culture where more people were questioning long-held assumptions about alcohol, and that we no longer had to choose between enjoying great beer and maintaining a healthier lifestyle.

The Rise of Alcohol-Free Beer

Had you walked into a pub or hospitality venue ten years ago looking for alcohol-free beer, you'd have likely been met by a raised eyebrow. At best, you may find yourself with a dusty bottle in hand; likely something bland and uninspiring that tasted like bitter honey (we all know the taste, right?). Pubs are undoubtedly woven into the fabric of social life, and rightfully so. The pub is an important establishment in society, a place we ought to protect and cherish. However, for decades, alcohol has been the lifeblood of the pub. Alcohol-free options remained an afterthought, reserved for designated drivers, expectant mothers or perhaps those with a doctor's warning to avoid alcohol.

But something has changed.

Alcohol-free beer has become more than just a make-do substitute for people who can't drink; it's becoming a choice for people who don't want to for whatever reason. The past few years have seen a surge in demand, with craft and macro breweries investing in high-quality alcohol-free options. Though once dismissed as a niche, often poor product, alcohol-free beer has grown in availability and quality and transformed into a booming industry, suggesting that consumers are not only ready for this change but are actively seeking it.

Why are more people choosing alcohol-free options?

There are a number of factors in play here. For some, it's about health; cutting down on alcohol will improve sleep, make your skin look better, provide greater mental clarity, and improve your overall physical health. Let's be real here - alcohol is basically a socially acceptable poison, isn't it? For some, it's a simple case of balance; being able to wake up on a Sunday morning without a foggy head, or savouring a well-earned alcoholic drink when the occasion calls for it, as opposed to it being the go-to drink for all occasions. There are, of course, the designated drivers, or the people on medication who simply can't drink; only now they are able to select a product based on their preference of taste rather than having to settle for whatever the venue they are in has to offer. There are also people like myself, who have chosen sobriety but still want to enjoy the social, sensory aspects of drink culture without the ethanol.

Studies have shown that younger generations are drinking less than previous generations. A combination of wellness trends, mental health awareness, and a desire for more control over one's life has led to a shift in attitude towards alcohol. We are also living in a digital age where any embarrassing act you may partake in when under the influence of alcohol will likely be documented and later torment you (trust me, those videos don't get any kinder when you watch them back after a few years). 'Mindful drinking', 'Sober Curious', and 'Zebra Striping' (the practice of switching between an alcoholic beverage and a non-alcoholic option during the course of an evening) have become part of mainstream conversation.

As individuals make this shift, naturally, the industry has adapted. Restaurants, pubs, bars and cocktail lounges now offer extensive alcohol-free menus. Supermarket shelf space for alcohol-free beverages has expanded. Bottle shops have a range of bespoke products for consumers to try. Multiple online retailers have appeared exclusively offering alcohol-free options and breweries are proudly advertising their alcohol-free creations, not as second-rate substitutes but as premium options in their own right.

Breaking the stigma

Despite this progress, there is, of course, a lingering stigma attached to non-drinkers. Alcohol remains the only drug you feel the need to justify avoiding. Alcohol has long been linked to celebration and relaxation. It is seen by most as a well-earned treat, so the notion that alcohol should be anything but the default is still often met with shock and occasionally outrage. Did you know that historically, Caesars would drink water from amethyst goblets so it would pass as wine? This is basically an ancient version of Guinness 0 in a Guinness glass. It also highlights how deep-rooted the stigma is; if Caesars felt the need to disguise their drink, you can see why some people worry about their decision not to consume alcohol in social settings.

But, that's changing.

More people are realising that enjoying a drink doesn't have to mean consuming alcohol. Alcohol-free beer allows people to participate in social rituals without feeling left out or pressured. I've experienced this shift firsthand. In my early days of sobriety, I worried about standing out, that social occasions would be tainted, that I would no longer belong in the venues I had once called home. As alcohol-free beer has become more available and more acceptable within society, I've felt those barriers diminish. Less often do I now find myself explaining my reasons for not drinking; instead, I can reach for an alcohol-free beer and feel every bit as part of the furniture as I did during my regular drinking days.

What this book is (and what it's not)

This is NOT a book that will tell you to stop drinking alcohol altogether. If you're somebody who can maintain a healthy relationship with alcohol and simply want to explore the ever-growing range of tasty AF beverages out there, then good for you (I'm so jealous of you, how do you do it?). I'm not here to lecture you, to wag my finger at you, or to tell you that alcohol is the root cause of all evil.

This *is* a book about alcohol-free beer (if you know me, that will come as no shock because it's literally the only thing I talk about). We'll have a look at where it came from, how it's made, which ones are worth drinking, which ones are awful (I'm looking at you, Becks Blue), and how it fits into a world that still mostly revolves around alcohol.

I'll share my own experiences, some good, some bad, and some outright bizarre. I'll give honest takes on some of the best and worst beers out there, I'll talk about the social side of things (you know how to deal with your dad's mates who still don't understand why you'd drink a beer without alcohol).

Most of all, this book is meant to be fun. Because, if I've learned anything from this journey, it's that there is a whole new world of incredible beer out there waiting to be sampled, and that sobriety doesn't have to be dull and flavourless.

A Quick Note About Terminology

Before we get started, you may be wondering what alcohol-free beer technically is. Different countries have different rules (remember the banana, that will be handy later on), but generally:

- **0.0% Beer** - Completely alcohol-free
- **0.5% Beer** - Technically 'low alcohol' if you're in the UK but legally considered alcohol-free in many places; it also can't get you drunk (again, the banana, remember the banana).
- **"Low-Alcohol Beer"** - Can be anywhere from 0.5% to around 3%

For this book, when I say "alcohol-free beer," I'm mostly talking about 0.0% and 0.5% beers. You know, the ones you can say "yes, officer, I've had twelve beers" and not worry about jail time.

This isn't a book about why you should quit drinking; it's a book about choices. About expanding possibilities rather than limiting them. Before we begin, it's important to stress something: we are, of course, going to be discussing various brands within these pages. I will be sharing my own personal opinion on certain beers; for example, Heineken 0% is terrible. This doesn't mean you might not love it; it would be pretty boring if we all loved the same thing, wouldn't it? So take my own opinions as just that, opinions. With that being said, let's dive in.

1 A BRIEF HISTORY OF ALCOHOL-FREE BEER

You may think that alcohol-free beer is a modern innovation, but you'd be wrong. Alcohol-free beer, in fact, boasts a rich and varied history, spanning ancient civilisations, medieval practices, and significant socio-political movements. For as long as humans have been brewing beer, they've also been brewing less boozy stuff— sometimes intentionally, sometimes by accident. We're going to take a little look (and I really do mean little because I'm no historian and my attention span isn't the best) into the history of these brews, in the spirit of honouring all of the weird, wonderful, and slightly questionable attempts at alcohol-free beer throughout history.

It's important to remember here that beer is one of the oldest drinks in human history— older than the written language, money, and even some of the world's major religions. We are learning more and more about the history of ancient brews with every year; however, we do have a fairly good idea of what the brews would have been like.

Ancient Origins: The Birth of Low-Alcohol Beer

According to ancient Sumerian legend, the goddess Ninkasi discovered beer. Ninkasi was gathering grains when she discovered that they had begun to ferment in the rain, turning into beer. She went on to share this discovery with humanity, teaching them to brew beer. This became a staple in the ancient Sumerian diet, as they believed beer to be a gift from the gods.

Recent reviews of ancient Sumerian practices have suggested that this beer may have indeed been alcohol-free, though how the brew was made remains a mystery. The brewing process involved fermenting cereals; however, the exact conditions and methods are unclear. Historian Peter Damerow reviewed archaeological findings and ancient texts, concluding that it was possible that variations in fermentation time, temperature, and ingredients could have resulted in beer with little to no alcohol content, although our limited knowledge of Sumerian brewing techniques presents a level of uncertainty.

There have been recreation attempts of Sumerian beer based on interpretations of the 'Hym to Ninkasi', which was a song of praise to the goddess as well as an ancient recipe committed to text around 1800 BC (though it is believed to have been passed down orally for many years prior), that have yielded brews with varying alcohol levels. Some experiments have produced beers with approximately 2% ABV, while others have resulted in brews around 4.5% ABV. These variations may suggest that the Sumerians consumed beers with a range of alcohol content, including some that were low in alcohol.

In addition to this, the dense, porridge-like consistency of this beer indicates that it may have been consumed more as a nutritious food rather than an intoxicating beverage. This perspective aligns with the idea that beer played a central role in the daily diet and culture of the Sumerians, providing sustenance and hydration, and it may indeed have been low or negligible in alcohol.

Similar narratives exist within ancient Egyptian culture. However, we cannot be sure of the specifics. We do know that the beer would have been consumed with a straw due to its consistency, we know that it had divine status, and we know for certain that the ancient Egyptians weren't sipping on a 0.5% pilsner while building the pyramids.

Medieval Europe: Small Beer and Daily Life

Move forward to medieval Europe and beer is still the drink of choice. Brews known as Small Beer were made for daily consumption. Again, there are contrasting narratives to the purpose of low-alcohol beer during this period (don't you just love history). It has been claimed that these beers were brewed as a safer substitute for often polluted water. The alcohol present was just enough to kill bacteria, typically less than 2-3% ABV. However, these claims have been disputed. We know that fresh water would have been available, with most medieval settlements being tied to waterways. There are various theories as to why small beer would have been consumed. For one, a small beer was less expensive than a strong beer, making it more readily available. Small beer was also a great way to up calorie intake during a time where labour was particularly intensive. Something that is not disputed, however, is the existence of small beer during this time.

And then came the monks. These beer-brewing holy men were masters of fermentation, crafting some of the best beer in Europe. But here's where things get a little wild; during periods of religious fasting, monks weren't allowed to consume solid food. Liquid, however, was fine. Naturally, they turned to beer.

This led to an alcohol-free experiment with some monks brewing extremely weak, watered-down beer to keep themselves nourished without technically breaking their fast. This brew became known as Becks Blue (it didn't, but I reckon it probably tasted just as bad). Still, if nothing else, monks were pioneers and possibly the first people to brew and drink alcohol-free beer because they actually wanted to.

The 19th Century: The First Recognisable Alcohol-Free Beer?

In the 19th century, things start getting a little more interesting, by which I mean we actually know a little bit more and don't have to read tons of historical papers to understand what may have actually been going on.

By this point, brewing techniques had improved and stronger beer was the norm. Some people, however, had begun to question alcohol's role in society, leading to the rise of temperance movements.

One of the wonderful solutions? Malt beer.

This was an early attempt at alcohol-free beer, a sweet, malty drink that had all of the ingredients of beer but wasn't fermented, meaning there was no alcohol. It was basically beer's awkward, unfermented cousin, like Days Lager. People drank it thinking it was a healthier alternative to full-alcohol beer.

The issue with this? It tasted awful, like Days Lager. Malt beer was weird, flat, sweet, everything you don't really want in a beer. It was as if someone had taken the first half of the brewing process and then stopped. Shockingly, this trend didn't last long.

Prohibition and the Rise of Near Beer

Onto Prohibition, where the American government decided alcohol was evil and banned it completely under the 18th Amendment. This ban lasted from 1920 to 1933.

Breweries were faced with what some might call a spot of turbulence. What were they to do when their entire business model became illegal? Some were forced to shut down, others got creative.

This was the birth of Near Beer.

Near Beer was legally required to be less than 0.5% ABV, making it technically alcohol-free. This would be the first time 0.5% ABV would be recognised as an acceptable level of alcohol within an alcohol-free drink, though if my dad's friends were around during Prohibition in America, they would have probably argued otherwise (the banana, I promise we're getting to it). The government thought this limit would keep people happy while still enforcing Prohibition. A number of established brands such as Anheuser-Busch, Pabst, and Miller Brewing Company released near beers alongside extensive marketing campaigns. Some breweries even started selling near beer with instructions on how to *accidentally* let it ferment at home, because of course they did. People would get creative in other ways with near beer, a common trick being to sneak a shot of alcohol into the beers to turn them back into the real thing. Regardless, near beer stuck around, and is really where modern alcohol-free beer began.

A similar shift happened in Europe during the Second World War, when rationing and supply shortages made full-strength beer harder to produce. Low-alcohol beers gained popularity out of necessity, laying the groundwork for future alcohol-free brewing advancements.

The 20th Century's Fantastic Alcohol-Free Beer Ideas

They weren't fantastic, they were awful. After Prohibition and wartime shortages came to an end, demand for alcohol-free beer magically went away. There were still, however, some rather questionable attempts to make it work.

Some of my favourites:
- **Attempts to sell alcohol-free beer as a diet drink** - Because if one thing will make you lose weight, it's a good glass of watered-down lager.
- **Beer-flavoured soda** - Soft drinks that actually tasted like beer (they didn't).

- **Instant beer powder** - A dehydrated beer that you mix with water. I'll say no more.

It's not all doom and gloom though. The 1970s saw a slight revival, with German breweries, such as Clausthaler, pioneering methods to brew beers with minimal alcohol content and little compromise on flavour at the end of the decade. This led to a slight change of landscape with major breweries recognising the potential of the non-alcoholic market. Particularly in regions where alcohol was not consumed for religious or cultural reasons. By the 1990s, as technology had continued to improve and brands such as Clausthaler were becoming more popular, Belgian and American breweries began to enter the space. I should probably also mention Kaliber in this section, but I won't. Needless to say, in the late 20th century, health-conscious movements and advancements in brewing technology began to allow better flavours and a wider variety of alcohol-free options around the world.

My Own Unfortunate Experiences

As someone who has shared a different alcohol-free beer online almost every day since going sober, I won't pretend that these dark days are entirely behind us. There are still malt-based drinks that sneak their way into alcohol-free beer sections, there are truly terrible macro brews, there are beers with some really strange adaptogens added that make the beer taste like dirt (I say some because this doesn't apply to every brand selling beer with adaptogens). I've had cans explode, I've had cans continue to ferment in my fridge (when you've not drank ethanol in a few years, you really do notice it).

We also have the classic pub experiences. When your pourer will proudly claim they have a fantastic array of alcohol-free options before placing an Erdinger on the bar (Erdinger is fine, but it doesn't constitute a fantastic array). Or who can forget the classic alcohol-free beer served in a Coca Cola glass?

Regardless, we've come a long way, right?

21st Century: The Modern Renaissance

Today, alcohol-free beer is no longer a second-rate substitute. It's a thriving industry. With improved brewing techniques, diverse styles, and a shift in drinking culture, alcohol-free beer has become a legitimate choice for beer lovers. What started as a necessity in medieval times, a legal workaround during Prohibition, and a wartime adaptation has now become a fully fledged movement, driven by innovation and changing consumer attitudes.

We saw breweries like Becks (yes, I know) release alcohol-free beer, with a number of high-profile brands not far behind. In the UK, we saw brands such as Big Drop and Nirvana emerge as the first exclusive alcohol-free breweries. We saw the birth of Lucky Saint in 2018, with their lager being launched on tap in 2020. We also saw the rise of alcohol-free craft beer post-lockdown with brands like Mash Gang leading the charge. This has been reflected globally, with alcohol-free beer sales and production rising to all-time highs across Europe and America. New beers are being released constantly, and the rate of popularity is showing no signs of slowing.

We now see craft-brewed alcohol-free beer that actually tastes good, a massive array of styles from lagers to stouts to IPAs to wheat beers to sours, and everything in between. We also see dedicated sections in bottle shops and supermarkets, with the majority of hospitality venues committing entire menus to alcohol-free offerings.

Alcohol-free beer has a pretty wild history. Some of it was accidental, some of it was outright weird, but today, it's the best it's ever been. So, the next time someone scoffs at alcohol-free beer, remind them that people have been drinking this stuff for thousands of years, then they'll laugh at you for being a history buff rather than for your choice of beer, progress, right?

2 HOW ALCOHOL-FREE BEER IS MADE

At its core, beer is the result of fermenting sugars derived from grains with hops, yeast, and of course, water. It's a finely tuned craft blending science and artistry. When talking to alcohol-free brewers, you will learn that they often had to experiment in their early careers, using equipment in ways not previously thought of. The challenge in creating alcohol-free beer is, of course, retaining flavour and mouthfeel whilst either eliminating or significantly reducing the alcohol content.

Alcohol-Free Beer Starts in Much the Same Way as Traditional Beer. It usually uses four key ingredients:

- Water
- Hops
- Yeast
- Malt

The Role of Water in Alcohol-Free Beer

It may seem fairly obvious, but water is the foundation of all beer. This applies to both alcoholic beer and alcohol-free beer. Although it may seem bland, water's quality, mineral content, and treatment can profoundly affect the flavour, mouthfeel, and overall quality of a beer. In alcohol-free beer, water plays an even more crucial role in ensuring the final product is well balanced. Its composition can influence:

- **Flavour:** The mineral balance (calcium, magnesium, and bicarbonate levels) can accentuate malt sweetness or enhance hop bitterness.

- **Mouthfeel:** The clarity and purity of water contribute to the beer's body and texture.

- **Stability:** Clean, well-treated water helps prevent off-flavour and ensures consistency with every batch.

How Brewers Optimise Water for Alcohol-Free Beer

There are a few methods at a brewer's disposal to fine-tune the water they use:

- **Water Profiling:** Brewers analyse their local water and adjust it by adding minerals or by using reverse osmosis (we'll get to that later, don't worry) to create a blank slate.

- **pH Adjustment:** Brewers will adjust the pH level of the mash (again, we'll get there) to improve enzyme activity. pH can be lowered by adding calcium or raised by adding sodium bicarbonate.

- **Consistency Through Filtration:** Modern filtration and purification methods ensure that water is free from contaminants that could introduce off flavours. In alcohol-free beer, these flavours can be particularly noticeable.

Water may seem like the most simple ingredient, but the role it plays in the production of your favourite alcohol-free beer is crucial.

The Role of Hops in Alcohol-Free Beer

Hops are the hanging flowers of the Humulus Lupulus plant. They contain natural compounds that influence a beer's taste and aroma. In traditional beer, hops interact with alcohol to enhance flavours. In alcohol-free beer, they have to work a little harder.

Since alcohol contributes to a beer's mouthfeel and perception of flavours, removing it can leave a beer tasting overly sweet and feeling thin. This is where hops can come in to save the day. Brewers can adjust the hopping process in several ways to compensate for the absence of alcohol, such as:

Dry Hopping: Adding hops after fermentation enhances aroma without adding extra bitterness, making alcohol-free beers more fragrant and full-bodied.

Hop Extracts and Oils: Some brewers use concentrated hop extracts to amplify flavour and aroma, ensuring the beer retains its character despite the absence of alcohol.

Blending Different Hop Varieties: Mixing hop strains with various flavour profiles can make an alcohol-free beer more complex and interesting.

Different hop varieties bring different characteristics to beer. In alcohol-free brewing, the selection of hops can be make or break. There are entire books that exist purely exploring these varieties; we won't go into all of them because we'd be here all day, but two of the most commonly used hops are:

- **Citra®** - Known for its bright citrus and tropical fruit aromas
- **Mosaic®** - Packed with berry and tropical fruit flavours

There are hops from all over the world, some giving floral flavours, some giving herbal flavours, some giving peach flavours, some giving earthy flavours. Name a flavour profile, you can more-or-less get there with hops.

The Role of Yeast in Alcohol-Free Beer

These tiny, hardworking microorganisms have been making our beer bubbly, flavourful, and intoxicating for thousands of years. Without yeast, we wouldn't have beer as we know it, alcoholic or otherwise. When it comes to alcohol-free beer, as discussed previously, yeast plays an even trickier role. It has to do its job of fermenting sugars and developing flavours, but it also has to be kept in check so it doesn't get overly excited and produce alcohol. Yeast is to be respected. So with that in mind, I thought we'd give yeast its own little section.

What Does Yeast Actually Do?

At its core, yeast is a fungus that has an incredibly important job: turning sugar into alcohol and carbon dioxide through fermentation. In traditional brewing, yeast consumes sugars and produces ethanol or alcohol as a byproduct. It also creates a whole range of flavours and aromas depending on the strain and fermentation conditions. One of the hardest challenges faced by brewers revolves around yeast. How do we let the yeast do its job without producing alcohol? We'll get to that in due time; the important thing to take away from this is that yeast is pretty crucial in the production of beer.

The Role of Malt in Alcohol-Free Beer

Malt, my worst enemy and my best friend. Have you ever had an alcohol-free beer that tastes like synthetic caramel? Thank you, malt. Have you ever had an alcohol-free beer with a delicious roasted profile? Thank you (for real this time), malt. Malt provides the backbone of flavour, colour, and body in alcohol-free beer.

What Is Malt?

Malt is produced by germinating cereal grains (most commonly barley) and then drying them in a process called kilning. This process develops enzymes that convert starches in the grains to fermentable sugars (remember how yeast just loves sugar?). In traditional beer, malt not only supplies the sugar, it also provides a wide range of flavours. Depending on the malt variety, you might experience notes of caramel, toffee, biscuit, or even chocolate. The malt's contribution to body and mouthfeel is also crucial, creating a balanced drink that is satisfying to consume. Just like hops and yeast, there are a variety of options available to brewers. The careful selection and processing of malt in alcohol-free beer are key to replicating the richness found in traditional beers.

So, that is a very basic breakdown of the four key components in most alcohol-free beer. The question is, what do we actually do with it all?

Brewing 101

Understanding the basics of beer production is pretty essential before we start to explore alcohol-free variants. It turns out beer doesn't actually come from a goddess who got caught in a rainstorm; it actually involves several key steps:

Malting: Barley grains are soaked in water, allowing them to germinate. This will activate enzymes, converting starches into fermentable sugars, kind of like when you chew a piece of bread for ten minutes and it starts to taste sweet (that was my favourite biology lesson). The germinated grains are then dried in a kiln, halting the process.

Mashing: You know, like Mash Gang (more on them later). The malted barley is mixed with water that is as hot as the sun (not literally, but it is hot), creating a mash. Complex starches will then break down into simpler sugars, giving you a sugary liquid that is known as wort.

Boiling: The wort is boiled, and hops are added.

Fermentation: The liquid is cooled and transferred into a fermentation vessel, which would be a great name for a bar, I reckon. Yeast is then introduced, consuming the sugars and producing carbon dioxide and, of course, alcohol.

Conditioning: As the beer matures, it will develop its flavours and carbonation.

Packaging: The beer is filtered (sometimes), carbonated (if needed), pasteurised (sometimes), and packaged (this step is kind of essential) before being sent into the wide world.

That's a lot of science right there. I also didn't mention how darn good the whole process smells. Like seriously, have you ever been on a brewery tour? They should sell scented candles.

Creating Alcohol Free Beer - Methods and Techniques

Before we get into this, you may be wondering - why can't we simply stop the process after the boil and before the fermentation? Well, some people do; have you heard of Supermalt? A lot of early alcohol-free beers were made this way. The issue is the taste is often far too sweet for most people's liking. There are also a lot of other little chemical reactions occurring during the fermentation alongside the creation of alcohol. So, in short, no, that's not the best idea.

Instead, we look to other methods. These include:

1. Controlled Fermentation

This approach focuses on limiting alcohol production during fermentation with the use of:

- **Temperature Regulation**: Fermenting at lower temperatures will slow yeast activity, resulting in less alcohol production.

- Specialised Yeast Strains: Some yeast strains are less efficient at converting sugars into alcohol. Some will ferment simple sugars and leave more complex sugars unfermented, leading to lower alcohol content overall.

- A Shorter Fermentation Period: If you halt fermentation early, you can prevent higher alcohol levels developing. To do this, the beer is rapidly cooled to stop yeast activity.

Pros: Most of the beer's original flavours are retained as the process closely mirrors conventional brewing. Advancements in brewing technology and filtration have significantly improved the quality of low-alcohol beers produced in this way.

Cons: Residual sugars may lead to a sweeter beer. Achieving consistent alcohol levels can also be challenging.

2. Dilution

This one seems super obvious, doesn't it? I didn't actually think it would be viable, but I guess I'm wrong. The method basically involves brewing a high-alcohol beer and diluting it with water to get to the desired alcohol level.

Pros: I mean, it's pretty easy?

Cons: This is a pretty obvious one; it tastes weak and bad…

OK, that was a weird one, so let's swiftly move on?

3. Dealcoholization

With this method, brewers produce a standard beer and proceed to remove the alcohol through various techniques:

Vacuum Distillation: By lowering the atmospheric pressure, the boiling point of alcohol decreases, allowing it to evaporate at temperatures that will not alter the beer's flavour too much.

Reverse Osmosis: The best method to quote if you want to pretend you know what you're talking about in a bar full of your dad's mates. With this method, beer is passed through a semi-permeable membrane (which sounds like a good time to me), separating alcohol and water from flavour compounds. The alcohol is removed from the filtered liquid, then the remaining substances are recombined. Fancy stuff.

Pros: Capable of producing beers that will closely mimic their alcoholic counterparts.

Cons: Requires specialised equipment that costs a lot of money. Some flavour loss can also occur in the process.

Industry Example: Stella Artois utilises this method to produce its alcohol-free variant. They brew their standard beer and remove the alcohol, resulting in a beer that is pretty reminiscent of the full-strength Stella Artois.

4: Simulated Fermentation

You remember the bit at the start where I said about beer not going to ferment and it being a bit rubbish? Turns out in some instances, it actually can work. Nirvana Brewery, for example, employs multiple methods to produce their range of alcohol-free beers. For some of their stouts, they use a method that requires no fermentation, and those stouts are pretty decent. So I've included it here to give it a fair trial. Hop additions and malt extracts are pretty crucial here to prevent a poor-tasting liquid.

Pasteurisation

If you've been drinking alcohol-free beer for a few years, you may have started to notice longer shelf lives on your favourite cans. As somebody who throws away mouldy bread (which is a bit silly considering all of the other substances I have willingly put into my body historically), I have always paid attention to this. We know that alcohol is pretty good at keeping all of those nasty things that can get into a beer in check. Without the alcohol, we obviously lose this function. So what is the answer? Pasteurisation, my friends.

What is Pasteurisation?

Pasteurisation is essentially a heat treatment process that eliminates unwanted microbes, named after French scientist Louis Pasteur if you want to know. This process will extend the shelf life and stability of your favourite alcohol-free beer. It will ensure no rogue bacteria or yeasts survive post-packaging.

There are two main methods:

Tunnel Pasteurisation: This involves running filled or sealed cans and bottles through a heated tunnel, gradually warming them for a set period before cooling again.

Flash Pasteurisation: With this method, the beer is rapidly heated for a few seconds before being cooled and packaged. The temperatures reached in flash pasteurisation are higher than in tunnel pasteurisation. Flash Pasteurisation is also the name I would choose if I became a professional wrestler.

Does Pasteurisation Affect Taste?

We've all seen the labels, right? Unfiltered, unpasteurised. There has been a bit of a boom in unpasteurised beer in recent years. Some claim pasteurisation dulls the flavour, others claim that modern innovations have minimised any noticeable difference in flavour. Many craft breweries rely on other forms of pasteurisation, such as sterile filtration, using ultra-fine filters to remove potential contaminants, cold chain distribution where they keep the alcohol-free beer refrigerated at all times (which is logistically rather difficult), and by using natural preservatives. With lager, however, pasteurisation is often relied on to ensure consistency and stability across batches.

While pasteurisation is a highly effective method to preserve alcohol-free beer, it comes with a price, quite literally. In short, it's darn expensive to do. There are not many locations in the UK with the facility to pasteurise, so beer has to be sent off for the process to be done. For large-scale breweries who mass-produce, the cost of this process is justified. For smaller breweries, however, it becomes more challenging.

The Delicate Art of Balance

Creating a good alcohol-free beer is a very finely tuned process. Brewers have to consider aroma, mouthfeel, and flavour preservation. Aromatic compounds contribute significantly to a beer's character; the beer must have the appropriate body and carbonation to mimic the texture of full-alcohol beer, and of course, the flavour has to be there, else it's all a little bit pointless. Needless to say, there has been a lot of trial and error, and breweries have often gotten things very wrong (remember the exploding cans). Fortunately, we are starting to see the results of a lot of hard work, with alcohol-free beers now hitting the spot more often than not.

This, of course, only covers the basic fundamentals of brewing an alcohol-free beer. Remember, I'm no brewer; I'm just an alcoholic with a new obsession. We have breweries doing wild things with sour beers, adding cherries into stouts, the emergence of smoothie beers, all that fun stuff. Regardless, it's safe to say that the production of alcohol-free beer has come a long way since the days of small beer.

Types of Alcohol-Free Beer

All beers, alcoholic or alcohol-free, fall into one of three categories: Lagers, Ales, or Wild (like a sour or gose). Within these three categories are a range of sub-categories. These categories aren't a measure of taste alone; they're defined by the yeast used during fermentation, the fermentation temperature, and the brewing process itself. Having a basic understanding of these categories can help you appreciate why certain alcohol-free beers taste the way they do and why some styles are much harder to replicate without the alcohol than others. Below, we'll break down the three categories and have a little look at their flavour profiles. The best thing about this is we could be talking about full-alcohol beer *or* alcohol-free beer. An alcohol-free pilsner is aiming to achieve the same flavour profile as a full-alcohol pilsner after all; else, it would be a pretty pointless endeavour, wouldn't it? Speaking of pilsners, let's start with...

Lagers

The most widely consumed beer style in the world. There have been entire books dedicated to the stuff. I could go on a tangent here as to why I love lager so much, but I'll stay on topic. There are many different styles of lager, from Pilsners to Helles. There are lagers my dad's mates can't get enough of and lagers that they'd turn their noses up at (can you guess which lager they love?), regardless, they are all lagers just the same. So what makes a lager a lager? It comes down to bottom-fermenting yeasts that work best at lower temperatures. This slower, cooler fermentation process results in clean, crisp beer with fewer fruity or spicy notes than ales.

Alcohol-free lagers are popular because they are naturally light and refreshing. They are also very easy to get wrong. There are a few factors in play here. With a lager, we don't rely on hops to add extra flavour. If a lager isn't spot on, it's very difficult to hide that. Everybody knows what a good lager should taste like, whereas a juicy pale can be left to one's interpretation a little more. Some lagers can also feel a little thinner than their alcoholic counterparts, as alcohol contributes to a beer's body and mouthfeel.

Common Lager Styles:

Pilsner

Originating in Pilsen in the 1840s, this is a lager that changed the world. Bright, bitter, and refreshing.

Typical Flavours: Floral hops, light malt, a dry finish

There are a number of sub-styles in this category, such as the **Bohemian pilsner**, which is softer, rounder, and slightly sweet, and the **German pilsner**, which is drier and more hop-forward.

Helles

German for "light". Helles is like the more relaxed sibling of the pilsner - less bitter, more malty, and endlessly drinkable.

Typical Flavours: Sweet grain, floral hops, smooth finish

Vienna Lager

Originating in Austria but now brewed widely in Mexico, Vienna lagers are amber-coloured with a toasty malt profile.

Typical Flavours: Caramel, biscuit, light toast, mild bitterness

Dunkel

German for "dark", Dunkel is smooth, malty, and complex. Although it looks like a heavy drink due to its dark colour, it's more rich and mellow.

Typical Flavours: Bread crust, toffee, chocolate, nuts

Bock

Bocks are big, malty German lagers, traditionally brewed for the end of winter.

Typical Flavours: Rich malt, caramel, dried fruit

American Lager

This is a lager most of us know, which is why I put it right in the middle of the pile. It's light, carbonated, and subtle. An easy-drinking beer that is often more about refreshment than flavour.

Typical Flavours: Mild grain, low bitterness

India Pale Lager (IPL)

A modern craft creation taking the hop-forward aggression of an IPA (we're getting to that), fermenting it with lager yeast, resulting in a crisp, bitter hybrid.

Typical Flavours: Citrus, pine, tropical fruit, clean finish

Dry/Japanese-style lagers

Did you know that Japan has the second-largest consumption of alcohol-free beer worldwide? That's a pointless fact but a fact nonetheless. Anyway, Japanese-style lagers are dry, crisp, and delicate. These lagers will often use rice to lighten the body and sharpen the finish.

Typical Flavours: Crisp, slightly sweet rice notes, floral hops

Carling

The lager my dad's mates like to drink.

Typical Flavours: Carling

Lagers are composed and refined, but that doesn't make them boring. From the bready warmth of a dunkel to the crisp bitterness of a German pilsner, lagers offer depth and diversity. Ales, however, are a little louder when it comes to self-expression.

Ales

This category also boasts a wide array of beers under the blanket term. Ales are fermented with top-fermenting yeast that work better in warmer conditions. This results in more complex, expressive flavour profiles. Hop-forward beers like IPAs are having a real moment currently in the world of alcohol-free beer, with the intense bitterness and citrusy aromas providing a strong backbone for flavour, compensating for the missing alcohol. Likewise, dark ales can retain their rich roasty flavours when brewed to be alcohol-free. Stronger ales can be harder to replicate, traditionally known for their big, boozy flavour (delicious yes, but we don't drink that anymore, do we, Ben?).

Common Ale Styles:

Pale Ale

Pale ales are a friendly middle ground. Balanced, gentle, hoppy and completely smashable. Originally brewed in England, they are the baseline for many modern craft beers.

Typical Flavours: Citrus, floral hops, biscuity malt

India Pale Ale

The classic IPA. Born in Britain, popularised in America and now more available than varieties of Walkers crisps in your local supermarket. IPAs are bold, bitter and absolutely dripping with hops.

Typical Flavours: Pine, grapefruit, tropical fruit

With IPAs come a number of sub-styles such as the **Session IPA** and the **Double IPA (DIPA)**. These two styles generally relate to ABV, with Session IPAs tending to be lower in ABV than a standard IPA and DIPAs being relatively high in ABV. For this article, we can mostly ignore these two styles, though there have been a number of DIPAs in the alcohol-free market in recent years. In an alcohol-free DIPA, you would basically expect everything from your standard alcohol-free IPA but turned up to eleven. A juice bomb, so to speak.

Two other sub-styles of the IPA, affecting flavour profile more than ABV, are the **West Coast IPA**, which is dry, bitter and clear, and the **New England IPA (NEIPA)**, which is hazy, juicy and smooth.

Bitter

My favourite beer of all time. Subtle, smooth and delicious. In my opinion, alcohol-free bitters have a way to go. Most on the market are relatively lacklustre in my eyes, although as I have said, it is my favourite beer style in the world, so my expectations are probably far too high.

Typical Flavours: Caramel, toffee, earthy hops

Brown Ale

Rich and nutty, brown ales bring in roasted malts without going full stout. Think toasted bread, coffee and a gentle sweetness.

Typical Flavours: Nutty, Chocolatey, lightly roasted

Red Ale / Amber Ale

Red ales have a beautiful reddish hue and a balance of malt sweetness and hop bitterness.

Typical Flavours: Caramel toffee, slight fruitiness

Saison / Farmhouse Ale

Born in the Belgian countryside, saisons were traditionally brewed in the winter to be drank by farm workers when summer arrived. They're dry, spicy and, for lack of a better word, a little funky.

Typical Flavours: Peppery, fruity, dry, occasionally sour

Golden Ale / Blonde Ale

Bright, easy-drinking and a potential gateway beer for lager lovers looking to broaden their horizons. Less bitter than a pale ale, but still with a hint of hop flavour.

Typical Flavours: Light malt, citrus, floral hops

Porter and Stout

Yes, these are ales too! Though often lumped into their own category, stouts and porters are technically ales, brewed with top-fermenting yeast just like the rest of the gang.

Typical Flavours: Coffee, chocolate, roasted barley

I would love to add mild to this section, but in all my years drinking this stuff, I've only been lucky enough to find one good mild. It was a collab brew between Mash Gang and Boxcar that is no longer being brewed (we'll get to that later).

If lagers are clean-cut and cool, ales are the expressive artists (wild beers are the child we don't quite understand, so just let them express themselves as they see fit). Whether you like things light and citrusy or dark and toasty, there's an ale style out there for you.

Wild Beer

As the name suggests, these are pretty wild. They're usually sour. These beers are often made with wild yeasts and bacteria (it sounds gross, but we drink those little yoghurts to stay healthy, so remember that). They will also be brewed in a mixed fermentation, using different yeasts in creative ways. For example, one could use a lager yeast but ferment at an ale-specific temperature. It's pretty experimental and not for everyone, like jazz brewing; only instead of using pianos, etc., we're using science.

This style of brewing in the alcohol-free world is interesting. Many alcohol-free sour beers rely on tartness and fruitiness rather than alcohol for their complexity, meaning when they are done right, they can be incredibly close in flavour to their alcoholic counterparts; however, when done wrong, you're basically left with a fruit smoothie (which is delicious, yes, but not really a beer).

Common Wild Beer Styles

Lambic

Lambics are brewed in Belgium's Pajottenland region using spontaneous fermentation. That essentially means leaving the beer to cool in shallow, open-air vessels where wild microbes can do their thing.

Typical Flavours: Tart, dry, funky with a cider-like edge

There are some sub-styles within this category, such as **Gueuze**, which is a blend of young and old lambics and fruit lambics (like Kriek), refermented with fruit, typically raspberries or cherries.

Berliner Weisse

A cloudy wheat beer with a sharp sourness.

Typical Flavours: Lemon, green apple, yoghurt-like tang

Gose

One of my favourite wild beer styles. This ancient German beer is brewed with coriander and a pinch of salt to counterbalance its tartness. It's incredibly refreshing in the most confusing way; I love it.

Typical Flavours: Lemon (or your fruit of choice), salt, herbal spice, sourdough

American Wild Ale

These are pretty impossible to place, as each brew is different. Brewers will use wild yeast, souring bacteria, fruit, wood ageing, and a pinch of chaos to create wild ales.

Typical Flavours: Take your pick really… Probably sour though.

Mixed Fermentation Beer

These beers use a combination of standard brewer's yeast, wild yeast and bacteria to layer complexity. They may start as a saison, a sour or even a stout, but barrel-ageing and time will give them a touch of wild magic.

Typical Flavours: Balanced sourness, complex funk (also a great genre of music), wood, fruit.

So there we have alcohol-free beer 101. From the basics of brewing to a glimpse at various styles of beer brewers will try to create in alcohol-free form, we got through it together. Take time to understand the process but don't let my basic explanations limit you, there is a whole world of alcohol-free brewing out there to learn about and brewers are getting more creative every day. To quote Ben Kenobi, you've taken your first step into a much larger world. Use this knowledge wisely (specifically whenever anybody tries to tell you that it isn't "real beer"). Before long, nobody will be able to tell you that alcohol-free beer can't stand side by side with its alcoholic cousin. Which brings us rather nicely onto…

3 COMMON MISCONCEPTIONS ABOUT ALCOHOL-FREE BEER

My favourite topic! My personal favourite is that alcohol-free beer is a "woke drink". Whilst we can pass that off as nonsense, there are some misconceptions that do persist. These myths often stem from outdated information or a lack of exposure to the diverse options now available. In this chapter, we'll debunk some of these misconceptions about alcohol-free beer, providing personal insight and factual clarifications.

Misconception 1: 'It's Just For People In Recovery"

The Myth:
Alcohol-free beer is a vehicle for recovery and is exclusively drank by those recovering from addiction.

The Reality:
Alcohol-free beer is enjoyed by people from all walks of life worldwide. Yes, it can be a tool for those in recovery (hi), but its appeal extends far beyond this group. As a functional drink, alcohol-free beer can be enjoyed by athletes, people on medication, designated drivers, and so on. It also happens to actually taste good now. This means alcohol-free beer is far more than a drink of purpose. People can (and do) drink it because it's an enjoyable drink.

Personal Insight:
Have you ever gotten really into something? I'm talking so into something that you will notice people bring the topic up three tables away from you in a bar? That would be me and alcohol-free beer. You don't have to look far in most pubs to see at least one person with an alcohol-free beer in hand. I've seen it firsthand amongst my own social group, with a lot of my friends opting to zebra-stripe through the evening, switching between alcohol-free and full-strength beer.

Misconception 2: "It Doesn't Help People In Recovery"

The Myth:
Alcohol-free beer is a gateway back to full-strength beer for all who drink it into recovery.

The Reality:
We can't win, can we? It's either a drink solely for those in recovery or it's a drink to be avoided in recovery. The reality is that alcohol-free beer can be a fantastic option for those in recovery. Of course, this doesn't apply to absolutely everybody. For some people, it can be a trigger and lead them to want the full-strength stuff. However, for others, alcohol-free beer can be an invaluable part of recovery. From the anonymity granted by having a glass in hand to the replacement of drinking rituals, alcohol-free beer has its place.

Personal Insight:
Hi, I exist.

Misconception 3: "It's Not Real Beer"

The Myth:
Some assert that without alcohol, it's not real beer.

The Reality:
As we discussed in chapter two, alcohol-free beer is brewed using the same ingredients and often the same methods as conventional brewing. The primary difference between the two lies in the methods used to remove or reduce alcohol content. There *could* be an argument that some of the alcohol-free beers that skip fermentation aren't "real beer"; however, this does not apply to all alcohol-free brews seen on our shelves. The real beer argument is, as a whole, a lazy attempt to discredit alcohol-free beer. If you're still unsure about how real alcohol-free beer is, go and ask a brewer who has spent years of their life attempting to perfect the process.

Misconception 4: "It All Tastes Awful"

The Myth:
Every single alcohol-free beer on the market tastes bad.

The Reality:
Some of them actually do taste rather bad. Unfortunately, most people's first experience of alcohol-free beer will be from a brand

they recognise. A lot of these mass-produced supermarket beers have a lot to answer for, as they often miss the mark, leaving a lasting impression on alcohol-free beer as a whole. However, there are other beers out there that taste as good as, if not better than, full-strength beer that exists.

Personal Insight:
Look, I have drank *a lot* of this stuff. I have conversations with people about alcohol-free beer on a daily basis. When presented with the "alcohol-free beer tastes bad" hypothesis, I'm always curious to see what beers people have actually tried. Historically, these people haven't actually tried many (if any). The fact of the matter is, if one claims to love beer but not alcohol-free beer, they actually just love alcohol.

Misconception 5: "You May As Well Just Drink A Soft Drink"

The Myth:
Some suggest that choosing an alcohol-free beer is no different than a soft drink.

The Reality:
Alcohol-free beer represents so much more. It offers the complex flavours, aromas, and mouthfeel of traditional beers that are about as far away from sugary soft drinks as you can get. They are brewed and crafted to replicate various beer styles catering to diverse taste preferences.

Personal Insight:
If you give me a glass of orange juice in a pub, you may as well hand me a balloon that says ALCOHOLIC on it. I go to the pub for the pub experience. To me, that involves beer, alcoholic or not. Sometimes I am really in the mood for a good glass of coke, don't get me wrong, but when I want a beer, nothing else will fill that void. We will cover this more in chapter five, because I could go on about the social side of alcohol-free beer for... well, about a chapter's worth.

Misconception 6: "It's A Fad"

The Myth:
The rising popularity of alcohol-free beer is merely a passing trend.

The Reality:
The increasing demand for alcohol-free beer reflects a broader societal shift towards health and wellness. Studies indicate a growing number of consumers are reducing alcohol intake, and the market for alcohol-free beer has expanded accordingly.

Personal Insight:
Observing the variety and quality of alcohol-free beers now available, it's evident that this movement is more than a fleeting trend. It's my personal belief that people have always wanted more alcohol-free options; they were just always pretty bad. As the quality of the liquid has improved, people's willingness to drink it has increased. As the quality of the liquid is showing no signs of getting worse, I don't see how this will not be a lasting change in drinking culture.

Misconception 7: "All Alcohol-Free Beer Is Healthier Than Regular Beer"

The Myth:
All alcohol-free beer is inherently healthier than its alcoholic counterpart.

The Reality:
While alcohol-free beer eliminates the risks associated with alcohol consumption, it's not entirely devoid of health considerations. Some alcohol-free beers contain added sugars to enhance flavour, which can increase calorie content. Additionally, certain brands may include additives or preservatives.

Personal Insight:
Right, I'm no health expert, nor would I ever claim to be one. However, I'm pretty sure the blueberry maple lassie gose I drank a few days ago should not really be consumed on a daily basis if you're particularly health-conscious. There is emerging evidence suggesting that no level of alcohol consumption can be considered safe, with some countries actively discussing putting warning labels on full-strength beer. Alcohol-free beer certainly avoids those risks, but it is still a drink to be enjoyed with some degree of moderation (which I absolutely do not do).

Misconception 8: "Alcohol-Free Beer Can't Be Paired With Food"

The Myth:
There's a notion that alcohol-free beer doesn't complement food as well as full-alcohol beer does.

The Reality:
Alcohol-free beers come in a variety of styles with flavour profiles that make them just as versatile as full-alcohol beer as companions for food. From hoppy IPAs that cut through rich fatty dishes to crisp lagers that complement spicy cuisine, there's an alcohol-free beer to enhance almost any meal.

Personal Insight:
I once had an oak-smoked ale. If you tell me that wasn't delicious with a pie, I'll tell you how wrong you are.

Misconception 9: "Alcohol-Free Beer Is Expensive"

The Myth:
Some consumers see alcohol-free beer as overpriced compared to regular beer.

The Reality:
The pricing of alcohol-free beer varies widely, much like traditional beer. Factors influencing cost include ingredients, brewing process, brand positioning, distribution, and research and development. While some premium alcohol-free beers may be priced similarly to craft beers, there are also affordable options available. It's worth noting that producing high-quality alcohol-free beer often involves specialised ingredients and processes that can contribute to the cost.

Personal Insight:
I find this one rather difficult. Especially when you bump into your uncle in a supermarket who proudly tells you he just secured two crates of Madri (the full-alcohol one) for £20. The truth is yes, major supermarkets often do offer almost unbelievable deal prices on full-strength beer, but even if I were still a full-alcohol drinker, I think I'd take a can of We Can Be Friends IPA over a bottle of Madri, even at £20 for two crates. In my opinion, you get what you pay for. Knowing so many brewers as I do now, I see how difficult life is for them. How much work goes into the alcohol-free beer that they produce, how much power large companies have over distribution

networks. If you are savvy, you can find alcohol-free beer in bargain shops or on store reward card discounts. If you want to try some of the best beer in the world, a more premium price is included with that luxury.

Misconception 10: "It Is 100% Alcohol-Free"

The Myth:
The term "alcohol-free" implies the total absence of alcohol.

The Reality:
Alcohol-free beer often contains up to 0.5% alcohol by volume, so it is not scientifically alcohol-free.

The Banana:
Buckle up because this is mad. You may have read that last point and thought I'd been stringing you along this entire time, that I was going to drop the biggest plot twist in the history of alcohol-free beer, that I'd actually conned you all into thinking I was living a sober life whilst secretly smashing such a minimal amount of booze that nobody would even know I was doing it. The reality is possibly even more shocking (you know, considering I'm an alcoholic and pretending not to drink whilst actually drinking used to be my jam).

So, a lot of alcohol-free beer is 0.5% ABV, we've covered that part and I won't deny it is the case. ABV is the measurement of alcohol content, in short it represents the total volume of something that is made up of alcohol. The higher the ABV, the more alcoholic it is. So far you're with me, right?

A lot of people will question a 0.5% beer. You get the classic "it's not alcohol-free" crowd, and you get the people who aren't sure if they're allowed to drink something that isn't 0.0% ABV. When I'm presented with these questions and accusations, I often reach for a banana.

Did you know that a very ripe banana can range between 0.2 and 0.5% ABV? Some fruit juices are up to 0.5% ABV. Some breads can reach a whopping 1.2% ABV. Mind. Blown. Chances are if this is new information to you you'll be wondering if it's possible to get drunk by eating a load of banana sandwiches? That was my first thought at least (old habits, ay?).

As it turns out no, you can't get drunk on bananas. Nor can you get drunk on orange juice, or on a 0.5% alcohol-free beer. This is because our body will metabolise this small amount of alcohol before it can have any impact on our minds. You could drink ten alcohol-free beers in half an hour (I've tried) and it wouldn't have any effect. You would actually drown before being intoxicated in any way.

Here's where it gets really confusing, boring, and weird. Different countries have different rules on what can legally be called 'alcohol-free'. So, in the UK, 'alcohol-free' drinks cannot be more than 0.05% ABV, meaning our 0.5% ABV beers have to be called 'low alcohol'. However, the same 0.5% ABV beer can be made in Germany, imported into the UK, and be sold as 'alcohol-free', because the legislation in Germany is different. So I can drink a low-alcohol beer in the UK with less ABV (let's say 0.3%) than an alcohol-free beer in Germany that has 0.5% ABV? Are you following? Me neither.

In short, there is *technically* a little alcohol in alcohol-free beer. But the amount of alcohol in these beers is so negligible it cannot have any effect on you when you drink it. So I wouldn't worry about it, unless you want to get angry about something on the internet, in which case my DMs are always open.

Final Thoughts: Embracing Curiosity and Changing Perceptions

These are just a few of the most common myths and misconceptions I have had to address firsthand. However, whilst a lot of these ideas still exist amongst everyday people, it's also important to celebrate a shift in understanding. For too long, alcohol-free beer was dismissed as a lesser alternative, a drink for those who couldn't handle the real thing. In reality, the evolution of alcohol-free beer is a testament to innovation, quality, and a growing desire for diverse drinking options.

Much of the negativity surrounding alcohol-free beer stems from a lack of education. People are often quick to dismiss the things they haven't had a chance to experience or fully understand; it's human nature to be wary of the unfamiliar. For decades, alcohol-free beer was just that, unfamiliar. The low-quality options that were available provided a perfect base for these modern misconceptions to be born.

Every time somebody dismisses alcohol-free beer without a fair trial, they miss an opportunity to discover something truly innovative.

As more people learn about the care and creativity that goes into brewing these beers, perceptions start to change. The popular opinion is changing, not just within the sober community but from a wider audience that values quality, variety, and the joy of discovery.

I've found that the more I share my experiences and insights, the more open-minded others around me become. It's a reminder that education and exposure are key. By demystifying the production process, highlighting personal experiences, and celebrating the quality of modern alcohol-free beer, we can help shift the narrative from one of scepticism to one of excitement and curiosity.

In addition, increased media exposure has played a significant role in reshaping perceptions. This media spotlight not only highlights the superior quality of contemporary alcohol-free options but also educates a wider audience about the benefits and enjoyment of mindful drinking. The more people see alcohol-free beer celebrated by brands they trust, the more they are encouraged to explore it for themselves.

It's easy to be frustrated when we encounter somebody who dismisses alcohol-free beer out of hand, especially now we know the facts. I used to stay silent when I came across these situations. These days however I like to consider it an opportunity to share a little knowledge and enthusiasm. Encourage people to explore and taste for themselves because once they do, they might just find themselves pleasantly surprised.

4 MY FIRST THREE YEARS OF SOBRIETY

If you've got this far through my book, you may, even for a fleeting moment, have wondered why you should trust what I have to say about alcohol-free beer? Sure, I've talked about the history of the stuff, the basics of making it, how I'm an alcoholic who discovered alcohol-free beer as a last resort, but what does that matter? I'm no brewer, I'm no scientist, and I don't carry any fancy titles (although I am still trying to make the gatekeeper of alcohol-free beer nickname catch on). What I do have is experience. Real, messy, and often laughable experience of navigating the world of alcohol-free beer as somebody who actually drinks it. I had no real knowledge of beer before I began drinking alcohol-free beer. Everything I have learnt, I have done so in sobriety. I've sampled the best, suffered through the worst, and learned all the tricks to finding a good brew. So at this point, it feels right to pick up on my own journey, from the first multi-pack I purchased all the way back in the prologue, so you can come along for the ride.

The mixed box of beers I had ordered were gone far too quickly. Determined to expand my options, I took to the supermarket with the enthusiasm of an explorer discovering a new continent. What I found confused me. I knew what brands I wanted to avoid, only they seemed to be all that were available. There were a few exceptions, but most of these were 0.5% ABV. Remember, I was entering this world with absolutely no pre-existing knowledge. Nobody had taken me aside for the banana conversation. I made a bold decision. I took the 0.5% beer home with me and stashed it away like a naughty schoolboy. I had, of course, ordered more fancy internet beer; however, I had realised that most of this stuff was 0.5% ABV too. I decided to only drink it occasionally; if anything, I thought it may actually take the edge off withdrawal a little (it absolutely does not). Before the end of my first two weeks, I had sampled every single alcohol-free beer in all of the major supermarkets in my town.

Alcohol-free beer was already becoming a little bit of a compulsion for me. Not as alcohol had been, this was different.

Alcohol-free beer represented a life that I thought I could no longer have. I had hit rock bottom when I gave up alcohol; I didn't know if the majority of my friends would ever want to talk to me again, nor what my life was going to look like. This amber liquid, this little glass of joy, gave me something to look forward to; it made me feel like there were still pleasures to be found in life.

The issue was I had nobody to actually talk to about this because, you know, chaotic alcoholism kind of ruined my social group. So what was I to do? I took to the internet, of course, and decided to begin documenting the beers I drank on there. If nothing else, it would keep me in line with my sobriety; I can't be setting up a page about alcohol-free living only to relapse after all; that would make me look really stupid.

So, the Sober Boozers Club began. The first beer I discussed was Heineken, very intentionally. Here's what I had to say:

"Hi, hey, hello, welcome to the world of non-alcoholic bevs. I gave up booze in January 2022 and have since been on a journey through sobriety and all the wonderful things that come with it. One of those things, ironically, was craft beer. Before giving up the booze, the word of non-alcoholic drinks seemed like a dark and lonely place, but I was very wrong. The intention of this page is to talk about drink and living without it, and to shine a spotlight on all of the wonderful alternative options out there thanks to capitalism and people like me who nearly ruined their lives. Starting with the one non-alcoholic beer most people have probably tried, Heineken 0.0. It looks, smells, and tastes like a pretty decent lager, although if you're drinking it in a pub, chances are it's lukewarm from a dusty fridge. But leave it to chill overnight, and you've got yourself an okay time, by which I mean it's as good as lager gets, really. It doesn't have that bleak aftertaste a lot of non-alcoholic lagers tend to have either. Give it a go, I assure you it tastes nicer than Carling."

You see now why I thought we'd open with the history/brewing, etc., rather than opening with that nonsense? I wouldn't have blamed you if you had decided to put this book down and forget about it had this been my opening pitch. Regardless, this was the real start of my voyage into alcohol-free beer. It's a liquid that not only saved my life when I decided to start exploring, it's a drink that has gone on to *change* my life.

My life in the first twelve months of sobriety was about as cliché as it gets. I had a promotion at work, I got a new car, decorated my entire house, shaved my beard, and joined a gym. You know, all the stuff people expect you to do? I had been regularly posting pictures of alcohol-free beer on social media and had found a tight-knit network of people who were also sharing their thoughts on alcohol-free beer online. My involvement was that of a hobbyist; I had a little notebook that I would fill in when I had found a new beer that I particularly enjoyed. My focus at this point was on raising awareness of grey area drinking, coming to terms with my own addiction; the beer aspect of my sobriety was, as I say, a hobby. I would go on to document my sobriety, I thought. Alcohol-free beer was a part of it, yes, but the main focus was on my own journey.

As my friends began to cautiously return to my life, I was faced with another dilemma: social situations. Alcohol-free beer had been great at home, but pub visits and social gatherings? They had remained a mystery.

If you've ever ordered an alcohol-free beer at a busy pub, you'll know the feeling: the slight pause from the bartender, the sideways glances from other punters that you're sure you've noticed. The first few times, I mumbled my order as if I were telling a staff member that I had kicked their cat in the street. I didn't belong in pubs anymore, I felt. The only thing that made me want to go back to the pub was the fact that my friends finally seemed to enjoy my company again. There were a few conversations during these initial pub visits about my alcoholism and the steps I had made to tackle it. It was apparent that not only were my friends happy to spend time with me again, they were actually proud of me for the work I had put in. Before long, I began to look forward to these pub visits as social events; the fact that I was drinking alcohol-free beer became insignificant.

With this change of perspective, I began to gain confidence in pub settings. I realised that if I asked for a glass with my beer, the alcohol content within the glass would be unknown to any onlooker. As far as the everyday pub dweller could see, we were just a group of friends enjoying a beer together. As for the odd looks at the bar when ordering, I actually began to look forward to them.

So that was me for twelve months. My life was finally back on track. My social life was the healthiest it had been in years, work was going well, I had even found myself in a relationship.

The Sober Boozers Club at this point was for me. It was a little corner of the internet where I could go to see other people who, like myself, had struggled with addiction. I didn't ever see it going much further than that. This was until one fateful pub visit. The evening began as many others had. I picked up my friends (because I'm a designated driver by default) and we set off. We had decided to try a new pub this evening. When we got there, I asked what alcohol-free beers they had available. I may as well have spat at the gentleman behind the bar. His response was "We're not that type of pub". For me, this was a moth and flame situation. I asked the man what he meant and was met with the response of "we're a pub for drinkers".

I don't know why this particular exchange stuck with me so much. It was not the first time somebody had dismissed me for my choice not to drink alcohol. But in that moment, I decided I would commit the rest of my life to changing the perception of alcohol-free beer (because apparently I'm still incredibly impulsive even without the booze).

When I say I doubled down over the next few months, it's an understatement. On top of my standard supermarket trips and online purchases, I started to visit bottle shops, breweries, and pubs that offered alcohol-free beer on tap. I started producing videos for each beer I drank, uploading a new beer every day. I began to explore world beers, importing Polish, Swedish, German, and American beer (I won't talk about shipping costs because let's just say some of it stung). I started a podcast interviewing brewers and people within the sober community; I even wrote a charity single called 'A Nice Glass Of Alcohol-Free Beer'. When I wasn't drinking alcohol-free beer, I was thinking about it.

The rest of the story is one I struggle with a little, because talking about all the things I have done feels dangerously close to self-praise (I still think I'm a terrible person because of the alcoholism deep down).

Over time, breweries started to know me from my social profile. The alcohol-free beer industry was growing at a pretty rapid rate (great time for me to have decided to start drinking the stuff), so more and more brewers were reaching out, offering me beers and eventually asking me to pop down to the brewery to talk about the stuff. This all felt wild to me. The first time a brewery followed me back on Instagram, I almost cried, but stepping into a brewery to help make a beer? That blew my mind. I would go on to actually release a collaboration beer with one of the finest alcohol-free breweries in the country. To this day, I still pay websites a visit just to see my name on the bio.

There was, however, something that I could not have expected, even in my wildest of dreams; to win a British Guild of Beer Writers award. The irony of this isn't lost on me, a former addict, now completely sober, being recognised for communication about beer? It sounds like the set-up for a bad joke, doesn't it? Yet there I was, standing in a room with the industry's most respected writers, brewers, and critics, accepting an award for my contributions to beer communication. Though it was, of course, a personal victory, it was a sign that the beer industry is evolving.

Although things had been going well for me, my imposter syndrome lingered. Within the community of non-drinkers, my words about alcohol-free beer rang true, but in this setting, would I be taken seriously?

The night of the awards was surreal. I had spent years reading the works of some of the people in that room, yet as I say, I felt like an imposter. What right did I have to be here? Then, my name was called, and in that moment, something clicked. I was the first alcoholic in active recovery to ever win a British Guild of Beer Writers award. That fact alone spoke volumes.

It wasn't just about me; it was about representation. It was about the industry acknowledging that beer is no longer a one-size-fits-all experience in terms of alcohol. To me, it symbolised a shift, an acceptance of the alcohol-free movement as an important part of beer culture. The evening was made even more sweet by the presence of a gentleman called Martin Dixon, a fellow alcohol-free beer commentator. Martin had been one of my earliest sources of inspiration and has since become a good friend. Being able to share that moment with him was beyond special.

If my journey into the beer world had stopped at that point, I would have been happy. To me, it was mission accomplished. Although I cannot claim to have had any real impact on the change of attitude towards alcohol-free beer, I had been there firsthand to witness the industry's warm reaction to an alcoholic winning a beer award. Nothing could ever come close to this moment for me.

Then I was invited to Parliament. This one was surely a joke, right? Turns out, no. I attended a drinks reception on behalf of Alcohol Change UK, to meet with ministers and drink suppliers, discussing the harm of alcohol.

Stepping into Parliament, two thoughts filled my head. The first was of the weight of history pressing down on me. This is a place where decisions that shape the country are made, where laws are debated and where for centuries, drinking culture has been as ingrained as the walls. The second, rather amusing thought that entered my brain was that my alcoholism, my fall from grace, had actually led me to Parliament. All of the rock bottoms, the injuries, the mishaps and the subsequent sip of alcohol-free beer that began my sobriety journey had brought me here, strolling through the Palace of Westminster on a grey January afternoon.

Being in that room, speaking about my journey and the role of alcohol-free beer was another moment of validation. For so long, I had felt like an outsider, kept at arm's length from certain social spaces, yet here I was.

This is why I write, why I advocate, why I champion alcohol-free beer as a meaningful part of modern drinking culture. I had never set out to win awards, to release a beer, to visit such iconic venues. I set out to tell a story, the story of alcohol-free beer, its place in the world and my own journey with it. If anything I have ever achieved in this space helps even one person feel like they belong in the beer world, regardless of what's in their glass, then it has been worth every word.

Three years into my journey, it's safe to say I no longer feel like an awkward newcomer in the world of alcohol-free beer. I've seen the good, the bad, the deeply confusing and I've come out the other side with a well-developed palate and an appreciation for a good brew. I've been on panel events at beer festivals, given talks at breweries and held counsel with beer lovers from all over the world. I've learned that sobriety doesn't mean sitting on the sidelines, it means drinking smarter.

The journey, however, continues. There are still beers to try, bizarre flavours to endure, and pub menus to scrutinise. To this day, I am as excited to try a new alcohol-free beer as I was three years ago when I discovered all of these wonderful brews for the first time.

Whilst the alcohol-free landscape evolves and grows, the significance of it in my life remains the same, as important as ever.

5 THE SOCIAL AND PSYCHOLOGICAL SIDE OF ALCOHOL-FREE-BEER

For centuries, alcohol has been the glue that holds social gatherings together. It's there at weddings, birthdays, funerals, Friday nights at the pub, even those awkward work Christmas parties where everybody has to pretend that they have other interesting things to talk about other than office gossip. Drinking is so deeply ingrained in our culture that it's often taken for granted, until of course, you decide to opt for an alcohol-free option.

That's often when the questions start. They often begin with a classic "why aren't you drinking?" They may take a more subtle approach; the two most popular choices here are "are you driving?" or "are you pregnant?" Occasionally, we will bypass the questions altogether and jump straight to the "just have one" argument.

I find myself in a rather fortunate position here. With three years of sobriety under my belt, where I have very openly and publicly addressed all of my struggles, I have no issue with replying "I'm an alcoholic" when asked why I may not be drinking. It's quite funny how quickly the conversation tends to shift at this point, from a confrontational question to showers of praise for addressing my issues. I'm also very fortunate that all of my friends happened to witness me burn my life to cinders with their very eyes. I don't think any of them are keen to relive those days any time soon, so they aren't exactly going to pressure me into drinking.

Whilst I say I am fortunate, what I really mean is that I have a great excuse not to be drinking. There is a justification that is almost impossible to argue with. I'm not really making a choice not to drink; I *can't* drink. Being an alcoholic may as well fall into the designated driver category.

So how about the everyday person? If it's only socially acceptable to drink an alcohol-free beer when you are unable to have the real thing, how does one even begin to navigate social settings with an alcohol-free beer in hand?

This chapter isn't just about the social side of alcohol-free beer, it's about the psychological side of drinking itself. Why we drink, how alcohol-free beer fits into our habits and rituals, and how social attitudes are, in fact, shifting.

The Psychology of Drinking: What's in a Pint?

To understand why alcohol-free beer is such a big deal, we have to talk about why people drink in the first place. It's a social lubricant, a stress reliever, a way to mark celebrations, and everything in between. It signals relaxation at the end of a long day, provides a reason to meet up with friends, and for many, feels like an essential part of life.

But how much of that is actually about alcohol itself? If we break it down, a lot of what we associate with drinking has little to do with the substance and everything to do with habit, ritual, and expectation. The cold glass in your hand, the clink of bottles, the deep amber colour of the liquid with the flirtatious sudsy head, and, of course, that first sip. These are all clues to our brain, clues that tell us that we are doing something pleasurable. Alcohol-free beer taps into this very framework, offering the sensory experience without the intoxication. It's a classic example of associative conditioning. Have you ever heard a can open from afar? That little psssst sound? If I hear that in public, my brain immediately goes into overdrive.

Why People Consume Alcohol

Understanding why people consume alcohol is fundamental to appreciating the rise of alcohol-free alternatives. Research identifies several primary motivators:

• Mood Enhancement: People may drink to elevate positive emotions or alleviate negative ones.

• Conformity: Social pressure can lead people to drink in order to fit in and adhere to social expectations.

• Social Facilitation: Alcohol is often consumed to enhance social interactions.

- Coping Mechanism: Some use alcohol to manage psychological distress, anxiety, and depression.

ADHD, Autism, and Alcohol Abuse

There are also links between alcohol abuse and individuals with ADHD and Autism.

The ADHD Connection

ADHD is often characterised by impulsivity, hyperactivity, and difficulties with sustained attention. While these traits may manifest in various ways, one of the significant aspects is the tendency to act without fully thinking the consequences through. When it comes to alcohol, this impulsivity can manifest in risky drinking behaviours.

For individuals with ADHD, alcohol can offer an immediate, albeit fleeting, sense of relief. Alcohol temporarily dampens some of the sensory overload and anxiety that can accompany ADHD. For somebody who constantly feels overstimulated by the world around them, alcohol can be seen as a way to quiet the noise. This can lead to a cycle where alcohol becomes a one-size-fits-all solution.

Autism and Alcohol

When it comes to Autism Spectrum Disorder, alcohol abuse is not as commonly discussed, but it is no less important.

One of the most prominent features of autism is social communication challenges. Many people with autism struggle to understand social cues, engage in conversations, or form lasting friendships. These difficulties can lead to feelings of loneliness and social anxiety. These conditions are often self-medicated with alcohol. Alcohol can provide a temporary sense of ease in social situations, especially for those who feel socially awkward or misunderstood.

Similar to ADHD, people with autism may experience sensory overload; loud noises, lights, or textures can be especially triggering (not to mention when your partner runs her nails down your back, that one isn't fun). For some, alcohol can be seen as a way to numb the world around them, creating a space where sensory input feels more manageable. This coping mechanism can quickly spiral into abuse if the underlying sensory challenges are not addressed.

A Social Lubricant?

Let's try to break down some of this and see where alcohol-free beer can play a part.

We touched on the social lubricant effect earlier. You may be thinking alcohol-free beer cannot have this effect, surely? Alcohol changes the way you think; alcohol-free beer doesn't, so can we have the same sensation when drinking alcohol-free beer?

Let's address (briefly because I'm not that clever) what alcohol actually does to your brain when you drink it, because science is important.

When you consume small amounts of alcohol, it can make you feel relaxed. This is because alcohol suppresses activity in parts of the brain that are associated with inhibition. Alcohol will also boost our dopamine levels, creating that warm, fuzzy feeling. So far, so good, right?

This all comes at a cost, of course. A life without inhibition sounds great until you're climbing a digger in Amsterdam at two in the afternoon before being chased away by a security guard, or you're screaming at somebody in your friend's kitchen because you think they drank your last beer. It can also lead us to misinterpret emotions and facial expressions. The more alcohol you consume in a session, the higher your chances of feeling anxious. Heavy alcohol consumption over time can even lead to a decline in the number of brain cells.

At the far end of the spectrum, we have alcohol-related brain damage. This can happen to regular heavy drinkers for a number of reasons:

- Alcohol is toxic. When alcohol molecules reach the brain, they can damage brain cells.
- Brain cells can be damaged if your body doesn't have enough water; alcohol is dehydrating.
- Higher blood pressure due to excessive alcohol consumption.
- Liver damage caused by alcohol.
- Fights and falls linked to drinking alcohol.
- Heavy drinking tends to be associated with a poor diet, which

can cause malnutrition and can be harmful for the brain.
- The brain doesn't get enough essential vitamins because alcohol interferes with their absorption from your diet.

Social lubricant or social nightmare?

So, how do we get that lovely two-pint buzz that we all crave so much? What if much of that confidence-boosting effect was actually placebo-driven? What if by simply believing that alcohol makes us funnier, more relaxed, wittier, then we act accordingly? Turns out we kind of do.

Fascinatingly, alcohol-free beer can mimic the effect. The act of drinking beer itself, regardless of alcohol content, can be psychologically soothing. The taste, the carbonation, even the weight of the glass itself can signal relaxation. There is something about having a pint in your hand that makes you feel more at ease in social situations. When we get to the placebo effect with alcohol-free beer, it's an interesting phenomenon. The first time I drank a pint of alcohol-free beer on tap, I can specifically remember feeling a little buzz. So much so that I went back to the bar to double-check I had ordered the right thing. This can be attributed to psychological association. Our brains link the taste and experience of a beer with those warm, tingly feelings that come after a couple of pints. It also plays into reward expectations; everything from anticipation to social feedback to reward itself. All of these things release dopamine. You can condition dopamine release from lots of things. Sugar, salt, Belgian buns (yes, please), and of course, alcohol-free beer. If we have learnt to socialise through the consumption of alcohol, there is going to be a strong relationship between the drinking of beer and dopamine release. The brain is a powerful thing; if it associates a familiar ritual with unwinding and a release of dopamine, it may just play along.

Ritual

For beer lovers worldwide, it's far more than just a beverage. It's a ritual. From the ever-so-delicious 'pssst' sound of a can being opened that we mentioned earlier to the weight of a full pint glass in your hand. From splitting the G in a Guinness to wasting hours of your life watching Czech Mliko pouring videos (it's also known as milk beer, where the majority of the beer is the head; they're often sweet and are drank in one, like a shot). There is an unspoken camaraderie to beer drinking. So where does alcohol-free beer fit in here?

The Pouring Ceremony

I am yet to have a good alcohol-free beer straight from the can or bottle (actually there is one, I'll explain later). I'm 99% sure that this is mostly due to my own perception of quality. If we were to really break it down, then yes, the transfer of beer from one vessel into another is important, pouring beer into a glass will release some aroma, form a head that protects the liquid's carbonation, and all of that scientific stuff, but if we're being blunt, it just feels better to drink, doesn't it? There is something meditative about pouring a beer, the slow, controlled pour, the gentle tilt on the glass, the final flourish to create that ideal head of foam, it's an art form. The good news here is that absolutely nothing about this process changes when you remove the alcohol from a beer. I've had fluffy wheat beers, hazy IPAs, crisp lagers, and hard-pour nitro stouts. I've even had beers with a head so dense that it will expand above the rim of the glass like a soufflé. I have a range of glassware, and each style of beer has its own dedicated glass from the collection. You're going to think I'm lying here, but I genuinely got emotional once after pouring up a perfect German lager. Counter this borderline obsessive stance on beer serving with my tried-and-tested method when in active addiction (smash six Holsten Pils from the can as quickly as possible and try to remember which can I'm using as the ash tray), and I think it's safe to say alcohol-free beer is winning the race in terms of the pouring ceremony in my world.

The First Sip

The moment of truth. The liquid reaches your lips, there may be some light carbonation as it makes contact, tickling slightly as the liquid makes its way into your mouth. This is where the hop and malt flavours will take over. Or perhaps sharp fruit, even smoked oak. You swallow, is it a bitter finish? Is it crisp, leaving you practically gasping for more? Maybe you've been met with a little flourish of sea salt to counterbalance a sour gose? As you exhale, you'll be hit with a second wave of aromatics lingering in your mouth, adding another layer to the experience.

Sounds borderline erotic, right?

We all know what to expect when we have a beer. For most, that first pint is about one thing: pleasure of flavour (there's a joke about my alcoholism somewhere here, but I'll leave that one up to you). Alcohol-free beer can certainly hold its own these days when it comes to flavour; if anything, it can be more pleasant when you factor in the uncertainty surrounding it. You're far more likely to be impressed by something that over-delivered than something that is exactly as good as you thought it would be.

Social Bonding

Perhaps one of the biggest rituals in the world. The coming together of people through beer. I've bonded with countless strangers over beer, and I don't mean making new best friends when drunk (I do have lots of those stories for another time); I'm talking about forming a genuine connection through the medium of beer. Of course, this is not an exclusive rule for strangers. Beer is also the lifeblood of many social circles. Meeting your friend for a pint after a bad week, going for beers with a colleague who has had a promotion, taking your dad for a pint on Christmas Eve, listening to a mate rant about her family issues. Whatever the occasion, beer is granted the right of passage. This ritual was historically challenging for the non-alcohol drinker, especially when these social gatherings were centred around a particular venue. More recently, however, this is becoming less of an issue as venues are increasing their range of alcohol-free offerings. Rather than disrupting this ritual, alcohol-free beer in fact expands it. Now the sober curious, the designated driver, the early riser all have a seat at the table without feeling like they're missing out. The alcohol content is different, but the ritual of going for a beer remains intact.

A New Age for Pubs and Hospitality

Gosh, that sounds daunting, doesn't it? In actual fact, it's exciting. To all of the landlords already offering an alcohol-free beer on tap, I salute you. These venues aren't just catching a trend; they are future-proofing their business. Pubs can become places to visit for work, rather than coffee shops; they can welcome more guests by providing options for everybody. The way we view hospitality venues as a whole can evolve with more alcohol-free options.

Societal Impacts of Alcohol-Free Beer

For much of the above, we have been comparing alcoholic beer and alcohol-free beer within social settings. The reality is that the two will actually go hand in hand. Alcohol-free beer provides a bridge, not a break from tradition. The impact of alcohol-free beer in social circles is huge, but it also affects society as a whole.

A Healthier Public?

For a while now, the NHS has been politely asking us to cut down on our drinking. 14 units a week? Sounds doable, right? Until you have a minor inconvenience at work, or your car breaks down? Alcohol-free beer actually gives people a realistic, achievable swap. Do you remember that TV advert from years ago promoting cordial as the solution to the blandness of water? Alcohol-free beer is my solution to cordial... It's not about abstaining from pleasure, it's about moderation.

To get serious for a moment, alcohol misuse costs the NHS around £3.5 billion per year. It's linked to over 7,000 deaths annually in the UK. These aren't just numbers, they're people, families, communities.

As more people choose alcohol-free options, we *could* see liver disease rates decreasing, a decline in accidents linked to alcohol, lower suicide rates, fewer hospital admissions, lower crime rates, safer roads, reduced domestic violence, and an improvement in work productivity and mental clarity. If alcohol-free beer encourages even a small percentage of people to reduce their drinking, the cumulative impact is massive.

I'm not here to say that alcohol-free beer is a magic cure for all public health woes, but it's a step in the right direction.

Boosting the Economy

The alcohol-free beer market is booming. In the UK, it's grown by double digits year on year. It's not just the big brewers cashing in either; independent breweries are making waves, creating jobs, and sparking innovation. There has, in turn, been a ripple effect in marketing, events, alcohol-free festivals and pop-ups, new retail spaces, and e-commerce platforms. The most exciting part here? It's only just beginning.

Representation in the Media and Popular Culture

Increased media attention around alcohol-free beer is helping to reshape the narrative. We see alcohol-free beer on TV, on billboards, at sporting events, and on social media platforms (sorry). From influencers showcasing dry nights to TV characters skipping the booze without a backstory, representation matters. These shifts destigmatise sober living, encourage people to explore alternatives, and help to make alcohol-free beer feel aspirational, not apologetic. This media attention is not only helping brands; it's helping individuals feel seen and supported.

Mindful Drinking and Mental Health

We mentioned mindful drinking at the very start of this book. It's undeniable that there has been a broad cultural movement towards mindful drinking. At its core, mindful drinking is about paying attention. It's about understanding what you're drinking and, more importantly, why you're drinking it. For example, instead of drinking every single beer in the fridge on a Tuesday night before having to wake up early for work on Wednesday, I may have thought to myself, "Just one will do me for tonight." Clearly, that logic doesn't work for me because I'm an alcoholic, but for many people, mindful drinking is a great way to live. It's not about stopping drinking entirely; it's about bringing more thoughtfulness to the table.

Alcohol-free beer supports mindful drinking in a big way. It offers the sensory experience of beer without the buzz that can cloud your judgement or affect your mood. It's a way to keep these all-important drinking rituals while avoiding the spiral of 'just one more' that alcohol can encourage. Ask yourself: why am I drinking this? Is it for flavour? Is it because you want to be a part of the social scene? Is it habit? Do you actually want to get a little merry (that's fine, don't worry, I'm not the booze police). Alcohol-free beer helps you reset your relationship with those questions.

The Meal Deal

Recently, Sainsbury's began offering alcohol-free beer as part of their meal deal. This move sparked debate, with etiquette experts suggesting that choosing an alcohol-free beer during lunch could be perceived negatively. This seems like a custom-made scandal to end this chapter on, because the whole argument against alcohol-free beer at lunchtime revolves around our social and psychological assumptions on beer as a whole. For one, it shatters the brittle belief that alcohol-free beer isn't 'real beer', after all, why would anybody take issue with somebody drinking a beverage that isn't real beer at lunch? If people are happy to link alcohol-free beer to the full-fat stuff when they see somebody sipping a can at their desk, why would they not be willing to do the same at a bar? It also brought to light some of the misconceptions we are now well versed in. I had the pleasure of giving a radio interview on this very subject when the move was announced. It became apparent very quickly how little the public knew about alcohol-free beer (I don't mean that in a negative way, I was in their shoes before I gave up alcohol). People were worried that children would be able to buy alcohol-free beer, which they can't. People were worried about the 0.5% ABV (remember the banana). It sparked a real debate, which I love. Despite the controversy, Sainsbury's maintained that offering a variety of drink options caters to diverse customer preferences. I take that as the grand return of the lunchtime pint.

Case Study: Café Gollem, Amsterdam

I have been fortunate enough to visit Amsterdam a number of times. Each visit has been about as varied as you could imagine. From what we'll call adventurous endeavours in my early twenties to a much more relaxed city break in my thirties, it's a place close to my heart. One particular location has always been a firm favourite. Cafe Gollem. I have taken many people to this particular drinking spot in De Pijp. They have an incredible selection of beer, and bar staff who can (and will) talk you through every single bottle, can, or line they have to offer. I have worked my way through countless beers there, from Belgian tripels to cherry lambics. Visiting Amsterdam sober was on my bucket list; Café Gollem was the number one spot on my itinerary. By this point, I was more than confident in my ability to discuss alcohol-free beer in depth; if anything, I knew far more about beer as an art form now than I had on previous visits. As I walked along the street, towards Café Gollem, I felt a bizarre mix of nostalgia and dread. I didn't think I'd ever find myself here again as a non-drinker, yet that very fact had made me even more determined to go and have a beer there. If I can't walk into one of my favourite drinking spots in the world and ask for an alcohol-free beer, then I am the wrong person to be shouting about alcohol-free beer all over the internet, surely? This conflict aside, I was not even sure there would be any alcohol-free beer available. How would it feel to be turned away? Was I prepared for that eventuality?

The cliché ending to this story would be one of triumph, of alcohol-free beer pouring from every tap and hours of hearty chat about the wonderful selection of alcohol-free beers available. The reality was quite different. It's not that there were no alcohol-free beers available; there were, in fact, several from various Dutch breweries. I didn't feel judged by my choice of beer; I didn't notice any disgusted looks from anybody inside the venue. If anything, my choice of beer seemed to be entirely uninteresting. This threw me. I attempted to bring the subject of alcohol-free beer up as a topic of conversation to the people at the bar a couple of times, but sensed their unwillingness to engage in such a conversation.

At the time, this was disheartening. I finished my beer and made a relatively swift exit. As a sober person, it's strange how quickly you run out of "first times" – first Christmas, first birthday, first wedding, etc. They come and go, and each one feels like a significant event. Café Gollem was to be my most triumphant first time to date, I had thought. To recreate those perfect evenings surrounded by beer lovers, without alcohol, was something I had longed for, so to have been met with indifference felt incredibly disappointing.

In order to break down what this visit actually meant, I have to take the nostalgia lens off. How many of these previous visits were actually as magical as my memory likes to tell me they were? Did the conversation actually flow freely, or was I just an overly eager, drunk tourist annoying bar staff with a thousand questions about beer? We go back to inhibitions, and the lack of them when drinking. I'm pretty sure if I had sunk a few full alcohol beers and then attempted to spark a conversation about alcohol-free beer, I'd have been able to do so. As a sober person, however, I find it much easier to spot a person who isn't really in the mood for that conversation.

When I think about this particular trip down nostalgia lane today, I actually see it as a sign of progress. If we look at the evening in black and white: I went to a popular drinking spot and was able to have a good alcohol-free beer. There were no verbal jabs, no sideways glances. The indifference towards the drink that triggered me somewhat (yes, I know I'm a ridiculous person) is also a sign of progress. To me, an alcoholic, my choice of beer is a pretty big deal. To everybody else, it isn't (unless you're one of my friends who really, really, *really* wouldn't fancy dealing with drunk Ben again). The indifference was not a sign of ignorance; it was, in fact, a real-time look at the world I want to live in, a world where ordering an alcohol-free beer is as uninteresting as ordering a standard beer.

If you're worried about socialising without alcohol, I get it. I promise you I do. I won't pretend it isn't difficult to begin with, but if I can do it, you can too. Start simple, have an exit plan to hand if you need to, remember social events are supposed to be fun, and if they aren't then you absolutely do not have to stay there. Over time you will begin to realise that those who matter in your life will value your company sober just as much as they do when you're half boozed (more so if you're me). Alcohol free beer can be just as exciting as the 'real thing' once you let go of these pre-existing ideas of what beer should be (booze basically). After a while you'll find yourself looking back at all of those wonderful beers you have tried in the alcohol-free sector and smile to yourself.

6 HOW TO ENJOY ALCOHOL-FREE BEER

It sounds like I'm trying to get you to take some unpleasant medicine, doesn't it? I hope by this point we've established that you don't need alcohol to enjoy beer. You don't need to compromise on flavour, ritual, or overall satisfaction. But, like all things worth enjoying, it's about how you approach it. You can neck a warm alcohol-free lager from the can, sure. You can also eat a roast dinner off a napkin. What I'm saying is, you can miss out on the full experience very easily.

This chapter is your guide to making alcohol-free beer more than a substitute. Let's make it an occasion. Let's make it delicious.

Choosing the Right Beer for You

Alcohol-free beer isn't a one-size-fits-all situation anymore. We're spoiled now, and you know what, we deserve to be. Gone are the days of being handed a sad macro beer or fizzy pop. We've got a full spectrum.

The real question is: *What kind of beer drinker are you?*

We broke down various beer styles earlier on; did any of these sound appealing? If you're a lager lover, a hop head, a dark and roasty fan, or an experimental sipper, there are a plethora of options available. In the following chapter, I'll be sharing my alcohol-free beer memoirs, from a catalogue of hundreds of beers I have had the pleasure of drinking myself. Gone are the days where you have to pick one beer and stick with it for the rest of your life. Don't be afraid to try something new. As a full-alcohol beer drinker, I was convinced I was primarily a lager drinker; now I'll reach for a hazy IPA or a gose over most lagers.

Serve it Like It Matters (Because It Does)

If you've made the effort to pick a good alcohol-free beer, don't ruin it for yourself. You're allowed to elevate the moment (remember the pouring ceremony we talked about earlier, we're doing it again).

Here's how:

- Chill it properly. Some beers are best fridge cold (like lagers and wheat beers), while others like stouts or amber ales benefit from ten to fifteen minutes outside of the fridge before pouring. Again, experiment with this. There are some IPAs that I love a little warmer than others.

- Use glassware. I don't mean to sound pretentious here, but you have to make it an experience. A tulip glass enhances aroma, a pint glass offers comfort and familiarity, a coupe glass for a sour beer? That's just showing off. A perfectly poured beer in a glass is just special. Build a glassware collection, let yourself enjoy it. Beer, alcohol-free or not, is a treat, it deserves to be treated as such, and so do you.

- Pour it with confidence (told you we were doing it again, because it's important). Fun fact; you can be a little more aggressive with alcohol-free beer when it comes to pouring. This doesn't really mean much in terms of enjoying the liquid, but it feels pretty great to pour up. Savour it, tilt the glass at forty-five degrees and straighten it up at the end to create a good head. That's where the aroma lives.

I've made a bit of a ritual out of it now. Glass chilled, beer selected, I'm ready for a good time.

Pair it with food

Right, I'm not going to pretend to be an expert here because that would be an insult to people who do this stuff for a living. But, if beer can be paired with food (which it certainly can), then so can alcohol-free beer, just like my oaked beer and pie story (honestly it was so good). Alcohol-free beer still has the body, bitterness, and sweetness to make these pairings work. If anything, with no alcohol present to burn the palate or overwhelm the subtle notes, some could argue that it pairs better with food. Pairing beer with food has always been a sensory adventure, and there's a whole world of flavour possibilities when you combine the right beer with the right dish.

Start with the basics: lagers go great with light meals, think grilled chicken, salads, sushi. Their clean finish refreshes the palate without overpowering delicate flavours. Pale ales and IPAs, with their hoppier bite, are brilliant with spicy foods, burgers or anything with strong seasoning. Malty beers love rich, roasted foods like stews, sausages and roast dinners. The trick is essentially to match intensity: light beers with light dishes, bold beers with bold flavours.

Here are some classic pairings that in no way highlight how much of a terrible eater I am:

Crispy, salty snacks

- Try: Light lagers and pilsners
- Pairs with: Salt and vinegar crisps, scampi fries, roasted nuts

Hearty Pub Grub

- Try: IPAs and amber ales
- Pairs with: Pie and mash, bangers and mash, roast dinners (with or without mash)

Spicy dishes

- Try: Wheat beers or citrusy pale ales
- Pairs with: Chicken tikka, Thai curries, jerk chicken

Cheese boards

- Try: Saisons or Belgian-style beer
- Pairs with: Brie, blue cheese, mature cheddar

Sweet treats

- Try: Rich stouts and porters
- Pairs with: Sticky toffee pudding, chocolate torte, salted caramel brownies

Experiment with food pairings, try different dishes with different beers, do some research into genuine food pairings (I think I've demonstrated my basic hints are a little underwhelming, but they're a good place to start). I should probably also note here that I've been a vegetarian for over a decade, so if all of the chicken and steak recommendations don't speak to you, I assure you, these beers work just as well with a plant-based diet (I just think the Sober, Vegetarian Boozers Club may be a little too niche).

You can also play with alcohol-free beer in cooking. A steak and ale pie? Why not go for an oak-smoked alcohol-free beer (I will get everybody to try this combination if it's the last thing I do)? Beer battered fish/halloumi? Go for it. Mushroom Wellington with brown ale? Sure. Even a lemon drizzle cake with a citrusy radler. The kitchen is your chemistry lab, go wild! As a rule of thumb, if a recipe calls for beer, you can use alcohol-free beer in the same way as you would use full-alcohol beer.

Shaken, Stirred, Sober

Welcome to the wonderfully weird and wildly refreshing world of alcohol-free beer mocktails.

At first, the idea of using alcohol-free beer in mocktails may sound a little unorthodox; shouldn't beer be left alone? Alcohol-free beer is, in fact, a little secret weapon in the world of alcohol-free mixology. With its wide range of styles and flavours, it offers a complex base that can be citrusy, malty, hoppy, or dry. It's like a grown-up soda that actually has depth, making it a brilliant companion for mocktails.

Mixing alcohol-free beer in this manner also opens up a whole new world of flavour. It brings even more variety to the sober curious and long-time non-drinkers alike.

Different styles tend to lend themselves to different mocktail personalities. IPAs are great for adding complexity, wheat beers work well in summery spritzers, stouts work well in desert drinks, and lagers are great in light, herbal mocktails.

Mocktail Ideas

We're going to start with something a little wild. I've spent the majority of this book telling you that alcohol-free beer was a grown-up drink, to be enjoyed in the correct manner. I've romanced it, put the spotlight on it, and broken down its rich history. This first idea takes all of that and kicks it in the shins. I'm only including it in here because it's a concept I invented. It is, the alcohol-free sour American float.

For this, you're going to want to take a few scoops of vanilla ice cream and pop them into a chilled glass. Then take the most juicy, fruity sour you can find and pour that into the glass. Top with squirty cream and a glacier cherry for a little pizazz, and you have yourself a rather good time. I say I invented this, I actually just found myself watching videos of people making American Soda Floats for a few hours one day and thought I'd try it with a sour. If it works, it works, right?

Now we've got that out of the way, let's have a look at some genuine alcohol-free beer mocktail ideas.

The Beergarita
- 1 part IPA
- 1 part lime juice
- 1 part orange juice
- Dash of honey or agave syrup
- Serve over ice in a salt-rimmed glass

The Morning Brew
- Wheat beer
- Splash of pink grapefruit juice
- Garnish with rosemary or thyme

The Michelda
- Lager
- Tomato juice
- Hot sauce (to your liking)
- Pinch of salt and pepper
- Serve over ice

Hop Spritz (Jump)
- Pale ale
- Dash of elderflower cordial
- Top up with tonic
- Garnish with orange peel

Beer mojito
- Citrusy beer

- Mint
- Lime juice
- Sugar

Create your own mix

There's no hard science to this, just your taste buds and sense of adventure. If you enjoy a bit of sweetness, go for fruit juices, cordials or even a splash of ginger beer. Want something herbaceous? Try mint, basil or cucumber (gross). The key is balance, start with a base beer, decide whether you want to amplify or contrast its flavours, and experiment.

A few rules of thumb:
- Don't shake beer in a cocktail shaker unless you want a face full of foam
- Build your drink slowly and taste as you go
- Serve cold and garnish generously

There's a whole mocktail world out there, spicy, sour, floral and bitter. The next time you take a sip of your lovely pilsner, have a think about what else you could stir it into.

Final Thoughts: Make It An Occasion

The biggest takeaway is that alcohol-free beer isn't something to endure, it's something to enjoy. Make it count. Dress it up, sip it slowly. Pair it with your favourite people, places, and meals. Let it be something that adds to your life. Every time I open a can or bottle of alcohol-free beer, I feel lucky. Lucky to be alive, lucky to be able to enjoy all of these wonderful offerings. The real joy of alcohol-free beer isn't what it lacks, it's what it makes room for.

7 THE MANY, MANY, MANY, MANY ALCOHOL-FREE BEERS I HAVE TRIED

When I decided to document my alcohol-free beer journey, I didn't think it would last very long as I would surely run out of beers. Turns out that was nonsense because this is set to be the longest chapter in the book. Who knew?

Let's remind ourselves of a very important statement I made at the very start of this book before we get into this: The following is based on my personal opinion alone. Yes, I have sampled more alcohol-free beer than most, but my taste buds will be different to yours, which is a thing to celebrate. Just as you may love cucumber, whilst it makes me gag, I may love Belgian buns, which may not be to your taste (you'd be wrong, but you get my point). I'm not going to write an essay about every single beer. If I did, you'd probably fall asleep, and this isn't supposed to be that type of book. But, if I hate a beer, you'll hear about it. Equally, if I love a beer, you'll hear about that too. Fair's fair, right?

It's important to highlight that the world of alcohol-free beer is ever-moving. Breweries will release small-batch brews often; once these beers are gone, they're gone. Use this as a memoir, a collection of beers that may be available or may not; regardless, the following are all beers that have existed and are valuable additions to the alcohol-free beer family tree. This is, if you like, my own personal collection (mostly), all the beers I've had the pleasure of drinking to date (again, mostly). Close your eyes, run your finger down the list, see where it lands, and try to source it. It will be fun (I promise).

Some housekeeping before we start:

• I have no particular order here, but we will split it into three main categories: alcohol-free exclusive breweries, supermarket offerings, and a section we'll call 'Beers in the Wild', these are basically beers that are available but not in supermarkets. The beers we discuss will primarily come from the UK, though there will be some wildcards thrown in from further afield (hence beer in the wild).

- I drink a new beer more or less every day, so whilst this is every beer (I think) that I have sampled at the time of publishing, chances are I've doubled that by the time you're picking this book up in your local charity shop in 2032. The list will be accurate up until June 2025, marking three and a half years of alcohol-free beer drank in sobriety. I'd love to keep it up to date, but I'd have to print a new book every day, which would probably be a logistical nightmare. In fact, I've proudly declared this list 'finished' about sixteen times already before realising I had since received a further four beers that needed to go on.

- There will almost certainly be beers that I have forgotten about or that I haven't gotten round to that won't make this list because, for one, I'm just one man and, for two, I'm horribly forgetful. So, if you're a brewer reading through this list and your beer isn't there, I will issue a public apology to you at my earliest convenience (can you believe I'm actually writing a book? Me neither).

- As stated, there is no order to this list. This rule also applies to the three sub-categories. Think of these beers as sand in the wind; wherever they happen to fall, they will stay. It isn't a list of 'best to worst', it's just a list I've thrown onto a canvas (not literally, again that would be a logistical nightmare and I don't have a canvas to hand).

- One final thing, this is absolutely not a tasting notes list. It's a list of beers that have passed my lips with a little garnish of nonsense thrown in by me. I mean, if a beer tastes like pineapple juice, I'll tell you, sure, but if you want some real detailed tasting notes, go and find Martin Dixon (Alcohol Free World), he's your man for that.

Do these rules make sense? No? Didn't think so. Anyway, let's dive in.

Alcohol-Free Breweries

The following are exclusively alcohol-free. You can find some of them in the supermarkets.

Mash Gang

Regarded by many as the kings of alcohol-free brewing, Mash Gang didn't just shake the foundations of the alcohol-free beer industry; they ripped them out and put brand-new ones in. They have released beers that should never have existed, pushing the boundaries of alcohol-free beer almost too far. It would be impossible to write a book about alcohol-free beer without mentioning the Gang. Before we get onto all of the beers of theirs that I have tried, here's a brief history of Mash Gang.

Mash Gang were founded in the height of lockdown. As they so eloquently put it, some mates from a council estate had a crazy idea to sell alcohol-free beer. The idea came from tepache, which is a traditional Mexican fermented pineapple drink. Jordan, who is the man behind all of the Mash Gang brews, owned a tattoo shop that was forced to close as many businesses were during the pandemic. He began experimenting with the weird and wonderful, from vegan blue cheese to tepache, which became known as the 'pineapple beer' amongst friends. The rest, as they say, is history.

On a shoestring budget, the Gang got some brewing kit, came up with a recipe, and made California Uncommon, their first beer. They raised the funds (aka all of the money they had between them) to make 200 bottles, which they would sell through Instagram (outrageous). I didn't get a chance to drink this beer because I was knee-deep in alcoholism during this period of time; however, Alex, who was one of the co owners of Mash Gang, gifted me his own bottle, complete with a wax seal, which I have been told is the last one in the world (there's no need for you to know this, but it's my prized possession).

The Gang admit themselves, in the early days they had no idea what they were doing. From buying boxes that were too small for the bottles to trying to send samples directly to Tesco, they were very much learning on the job. Finally, Brewdog Old Street, which was the flagship alcohol-free location for the brand, offered Mash Gang a launch party. This presented another issue, they suddenly had to produce a lot more beer than they were used to.

They were able to locate a contract brewer, which is essentially like renting a brewery for a session (it's more complicated than that but you get what I mean), who could produce the quantity needed. This would be Jordan's first time on a 'real brew kit', having spent months watching YouTube videos, reading books, taking home brewing to the next level while seeking hops that would otherwise be going to waste from various breweries that weren't operating at full scale due to COVID.

They brewed nine beers for the Brewdog launch, with two of them failing, leaving seven beers. The launch event sold out. From this point, Mash Gang as a business began to scale, with bottle shops taking interest, although the beers that were sold were still being hand-canned by the guys.

Enter Northern Monk. More specifically, enter a chance online conversation with Northern Monk. If you've ever met any of the Mash Gang chaps, you'll know how infectious their aura is. They are a fantastic bunch of people with some absolutely wild ideas. So, whilst they will claim this was a lucky chance encounter, I can't see how it could have gone any other way.

Jordan had been working on a gummy worm sour (of course he was working on a gummy worm sour), which he sent to Northern Monk. They were impressed, so pitched a collab. This was by far the largest scale brew for Mash Gang at the time. It also opened other doors, like being able to use Northern Monk's facilities for brewing, and of course the massive stamp of approval that comes from working with Northern Monk.

This working relationship also presented a huge educational advantage. Working alongside Northern Monk, the Gang learnt how to fill in the gaps, essentially completing the puzzle.

Mash Gang would go on to bounce around between breweries, from Gypsy Hill to Fierce to Vault City, producing more and more beer, gaining more and more traction to the point that they couldn't keep up with demand. They released collab brews with pretty much everybody, with Jord sharing his knowledge that would go on to shape the industry. They launched in Australia (more on those beers later) and in America with Pilot Project Brewing. They even brought in a CFO, like a real business. He's a chap named Roger and he's one of the nicest (and most intelligent) chaps I've met.

In 2024, Mash Gang was acquired by DioniLife. This was huge news for the industry, and for the guys who had built the brand from the ground up. An acquisition of this scale not only legitimised the brand, it legitimised the entire sector.

That is a very brief history of Mash Gang; there are tons of stories we could go into, from exploding cans to shipping delays because of Somali pirates. Mash Gang, in my opinion, are one of the most important brands in recent years, not only for alcohol-free beer but for society as a whole. There was a time when you couldn't pick up a can of alcohol-free beer without seeing Mash Gang credited somewhere on the can. I arrived slightly late to the party, giving up alcohol in 2022; the Gang were already making waves. Regardless, there are countless Mash Gang brews I have been able to try.

Very Small Moose (collab with Fierce Beer): Imperial Stout with chocolate and vanilla.

Neskveik: Remember when I said I'd do a bit of a deeper dive on some select beers? I'm doing just that on beer number two. Neskveik is essentially a white stout, with strawberry and vanilla. It was a part of the Gang's weird and wonderful breakfast cereal-inspired range (you know, normal beer stuff). It has a special place in my heart. It was probably the first alcohol-free beer that really stopped me in my tracks. Never did I think when I gave up alcohol that I would be able to have a beer like this. Sadly, this was a super limited edition release (spoiler alert, most of these Mash Gang brews are), which is a real shame because when you really want yourself a can of Neskveik, nothing else will scratch the itch.

Sour Batch Hops: Another breakfast cereal beer. This one was a pale ale with red berry and candied citrus. It left a sour, acidic bite which was counterbalanced with sugar. Lots and lots of it.

Cryo Pop Tarts: Guess what, it's another breakfast cereal pale ale. This one had notes of vanilla and pastry. Also, lots of sugar (there's a theme here).

Stoop: American-style pilsner. An absolute classic in the world of alcohol-free beer. For many, this is the number one lager on the market. The first beer the guys tried to make, it has stood the test of time and left a lasting impression on people. There have been a number of renditions of Stoop, such as the **Japanese lager**, which was also excellent.

Nothing But The Snow (collab with Ridgeside): A cold IPA, taking elements of a lager and a NEIPA to produce a clean, crisp IPA. This was brewed with lager yeast at a higher temperature before being dosed with Citra Spectrum hops.

Get Wavy (collab with Vocation): Pale ale with tropical notes of orange and grapefruit.

Chug: Arguably Mash Gang's signature brew. From the iconic can to the explosion of flavour, Chug is a hazy IPA done to perfection. There have been a few variations of this beer make their way to our fridges also, such as **Chug Gold**.

ADHD (collab with Alpha Delta): Sour pale ale. Sounds weird, but it worked.

Gacha Squishy Supreme Sour (collab with Northern Monk): Okay, so this was wild. The concept was based on Japanese gacha machines that dispense random capsule toys. How does that relate to beer? Well, you would receive a random can, with a random liquid inside. The colour of the beer was also different. Cyan, magenta, yellow, you weren't sure what you would get. They could also be mixed together at home to create weird and wonderful cocktails. It was an outrageous concept and I loved it.

Sauvin Blanc: An experimental brew with wine-like notes, white oak and a juicy yet dry mouthfeel.

Very Mild (collab with Boxcar): If I could will one beer back into existence, it would be this. I have been searching for a good mild since going sober and this was as close as I've ever got. Unfortunately, Boxcar went into administration in 2023, which was a tragic shame.

Can'n Krunk: Oh look, we're back on the breakfast cereal beers. This was a pale ale with cinnamon and vanilla. It wasn't as sweet as its cereal-inspired counterparts, with a more 'beer-like' flavour. That doesn't mean it wasn't absolutely outrageous, it was.

Only In Dreams (collab with Vault City): The first Vault City collab we're going to chat about. Vault City, of course, is famous for sour beers, so who better to collab with for a top-notch alcohol-free sour beer? This was a strawberry and jalapeño margarita pickleback.

Mango Marshmallow Moon Milk (collab with Vault City): The second of the Vault City and Mash Gang collaboration series. As the name suggests, it was a mango and marshmallow sour.

Mangonada: Mango was clearly having a moment here. This was a mango, lime, and chili lager. There was also a little salt thrown in to hold the whole thing together.

Night Curse: Tropical IPA.

Like Icarus: The first Mash Gang wheat beer. This was what you'd call an American wheat beer (you know the sort). Orange and coriander came through, it was light, it was fragrant. Writing about it makes me want one, in fact.

Natural History: West Coast IPA.

Self-Titled (collab with Northern Monk): This was an American Pale Ale. It was also the first beer Mash Gang got on supermarket shelves. It launched in Morrisons. This was obviously a big deal. Being Mash Gang, they pushed to have it included in the full ABV section of stores, rather than in the no and low section.

From Devastation to Bliss: A fruited wheat beer, with a subtle red berry and Turkish delight aroma.

Reign in Blood: Chocolate and Cherry Stout. This is a cult classic. More on this later...

Stay Gold: West Coast Pale Ale.

Stay True: East Coast Pale Ale.

Hold Fast: Lager.

South Of Heaven: Just so you know at this point, we're not even halfway through. Honestly, these guys were absolute beer-making machines. South Of Heaven was a red pilsner. Slightly fruity, slightly gritty.

Rad: Tropical IPA with passionfruit and mango notes.

South Central: West Coast IPA, spiked with caramelised

pineapple, candied lime, and a little chilli.

Paradigm Shift: A very limited-edition small-batch IPA, brewed for Hop City.

Anxiety Saint: Coffee stout. This is another one of those beers amongst alcohol-free commentators that has a place in the history books. People absolutely loved it. It was one of the first alcohol-free stouts to really, really hit the spot.

Cheap Lager: Pretty much does what it says on the tin. A 'cheap' lager. Clean, crisp, smashable.

Birth, Life, and **Death** (collabs with Brulo and The Garden Brewery): These were three collab brews. Birth was a West Coast IPA, Life was a hazy IPA, and Death was a German-style pilsner.

Logik Kills Magik: Shandy/Radler or as they so wonderfully put it: Mango Bellini.

Unnatural History: Fruited West Coast IPA.

Help Wanted Nights: I loved everything about this beer. From the concept to the taste. It was a coffee and doughnut stout.

Too Scary: West Coast IPA with pineapple, passion fruit, and guava.

National Anthem: Cherry Cola Ice Cream Pastry Stout. It was pretty wild.

Hand That Feeds: Vanilla stout.

Vice: Super limited-edition imperial stout.

Virgin Blackcurrant Kir Royale (collab with Vault City): This was a sour beer with blackcurrant and white grape.

Sorbetto (collab with Pastore): I had a couple of these sours. There was an orange, vanilla and pineapple one and a strawberry, cherry and lime. When I say they were sour, they were almost too sour.

Low Lux (collab with Verdant): This was possibly the first alcohol-free beer that had a 'big release day' feel to it for me. Low Lux was Verdant's first dipping of the toe into the world of alcohol-free beer. It was a New England IPA and about as hoppy as physically possible.

ITPA: Iced Tea Pale Ale. Should absolutely not work, should it? It did, however. Once you had a taste for it, it was all you wanted to drink.

Baby Iris (collab with Harrogate Brewing Co): New England IPA.

Unlucky Charms: This was technically the first breakfast cereal-inspired beer Mash Gang released. I missed the boat the first time round, then they decided to do a rebrew. It was inspired by, well, you know. One of the most beautifully weird beers I have ever had in my life. It is now off the shelves, but they rebrewed it once, so who knows what the future holds...

Cult: Hazy Pale Ale. This has become one of Mash Gang's biggest hits. It's an absolute fridge essential.

Hawg: American-style Pale Ale. This was a trial-and-error beer. A fine blend of delicateness and fruitiness. I'd love to see this one reworked today because it had the potential to be excellent.

Low Life: This one was special. A light lager that absolutely hit the nail on the head. This may be one of the only alcohol-free beers I've ever preferred straight from the can. You know when you're trying to give up cigarettes, then you have that one that tastes wonderful and makes you question everything? This beer was that.

Colosseum of Light: Pale Ale with Idaho 7.

This Is Cowboy Sh*t: For a little while, Mash Gang offered monthly subscription boxes. Within these boxes, you would receive small-batch limited-edition beers that were exclusively available through this service. It was a great little bit of research and development. This beer was one of those sub-exclusive beers. It was a West Coast pale ale. Fairly zingy, extremely resinous.

Superstack (collab with Vault City): Blueberry Blackcurrant

Maple Sour.

Blue Blood: A sub box exclusive brew. This was an Earl Grey tea pale ale.

Weeping Somnambulist: Another sub-exclusive, continuing with the tea beer experiment. This one was based on herbal tea.

Never Say Never (collab with Wylam): an IPA with El Dorado and Superdelic.

Crystal Ammunition: Quite possibly one of my favourite alcohol-free lagers to date. This was inspired by American lagers (you know the one) and it absolutely blew me away.

To The Stars (collab with Vault City): A rocket lolly-inspired sour beer.

Pine Lime Death Shake: It's time to talk about Mash Gang Australia. This was a project fronted by a chap called Trent, who just so happens to be a wonderful human being from Australia. Trent had been running his own alcohol-free beer subscription box service before he came into contact with the gang. This proved difficult as there weren't many good alcohol-free options over in Australia at the time. He connected with the guys at Mash Gang and before long Mash Gang Australia was born. Just as Jordan had never brewed beer before starting Mash Gang, Trent had never brewed beer before starting Mash Gang Australia, which makes the beers he produced even more impressive. Pine Lime was one of them. A milkshake IPA with pineapple and candied lime. This recipe was brought over to the UK and became a sub box exclusive beer, along with...

Purp Slurp Deathshake: Milkshake IPA with blueberry, taro, tonka and vanilla. This one was not as good as the Pine Lime (sorry Jord).

Peach Mango Pie PA: Inspired by a hot, sweet, deep-fried pie from a fast food joint. This beer absolutely rocked my world. I forgot it had existed until writing this and now I want one more than I've ever wanted anything in the world. I hate this list.

Sinner Bone: A cinnamon stout. When I say cinnamon, I mean it. In fact, there was too much cinnamon. You either loved it or hated it.

Spiritual Industrial Complex: Hazy Pale Ale.

Do You Like Trains?: This was a sub-exclusive beer. This beer used Phantasm, which is a powder extract derived from grape skins. It boosts the release of thiols, giving tropical, fruity notes. This beer was awesome.

Furthur: An American-style wheat beer.

Call of the Void (collab with Siren): Nitro stout. Very, very, very good.

Out of Nowhere (collab with Siren): West Coast Pils.

Journey Juice: Produced for the USA, brought over to the UK. Sweet, slightly salty, a little bitter, it's a Sabro Pale with mango, chilli and lime.

Beach Goon: We're heading back to Mash Gang Australia for this one. Beach Goon was Trent's first 100% original recipe. It may be the finest beer under the Mash Gang umbrella. It never made its way over to the UK; Trent actually sent me his last can of the stuff. It's an IPA and I would pay good money to see it made again.

Dorsia: A sub-box exclusive beer. This was a concept beer, if ever I've encountered one. Based on fine dining. It had lime, yuzu, black pepper and, for the record, a beautiful can design.

Regulate (collab with One Drop): Mash Gang Australia teamed up with One Drop to produce this delicious Oat Cream Pale Ale. I had to beg Jordan to send me a can of this (writing all of this makes me realise how much these guys have given me); it absolutely lived up to its name. Creamy and delicious.

Parallels: Another from Australia, this was a West Coast Pils.

Gang Gang (collab with One Drop): This may be the best alcohol-free stout I have had to date, from Mash Gang Australia or anywhere else in the world. It was a biscotti pastry stout that lived up to the name. From aroma to taste to mouthfeel, this beer was everything I wanted it to be. A work of art.

Strange Latitudes: Daquiri IPA. This was like a beach bar in a can.

Siege Perilous: European pale lager. This was excellent. Mash Gang do lagers very, very well.

Cultra: This was weird. They took Cult, then they did some stuff to it. I asked what, they wouldn't tell me. It was still good, but weird.

Super DIPA (collab with Northern Monk and Commonwealth): This was part of Northern Monk's Patrons Project. Two beers were released, an alcohol-free and a full-alc DIPA. It was super limited edition and super packed full of flavour.

Council Pop: A product of Mash Gang USA brought over to the UK. IPA spiked with Phantasm.

Stoop Lite: Another USA brew. This is similar to Low Life, a light lager.

Beyond The Pines: Yet another American export. This is a West Coast lager.

Delulu: Tropical IPA.

Hot Rock Burns: One of my favourite beer names ever, also one of my favourite Mash Gang beers of all time. It was a dank IPA.

Architecture And Morality (collab with Cloudwater): This was a bit of a bucket list beer. A hazy pale ale bursting with peach and apricot, with a grapefruit finish.

Citra Is Putting My Kids Through College: Another contender for best beer name of all time. This was a sub box exclusive and marked Mash Gang's journey into one-hop beers. For this one, naturally, they used Citra.

Some Kind Of Monstera: Sub box exclusive, single-hop series. This one used Mosaic.

Serpiente (collab with Cervecería Paracaidista): Remember the Mexican fermented pineapple drink from the very beginning? This beer was a nod to that.

Ghost In The Machine (collab with We Can Be Friends): The first collaboration brew between two alcohol-free breweries (to my knowledge). This was a lager and something I loved to see as fans of both breweries (more on We Can Be Friends shortly).

Ruffian: Single Hop Series beer, using Nelson Sauvin.

Don't Be Sad Bro: Single Hop Series, with Sabro.

Chews Life: Sub box exclusive, a fruit salad chewie sweet-inspired Pale Ale.

Lesser Evil: Remember the chocolate cherry stout we mentioned earlier? Enter Lesser Evil. The first beer released post-acquisition, with a little name change.

Glug: Cerveza Lager

Dream Crush: The last sub box exclusive beer I had before the service was stopped. A fitting name. The hop used in this one was Superdelic.

Okay, so, I didn't think this section would be so long. I'll be honest, as I was writing, I did have a little look through my notes of all the other breweries we're yet to discuss and have a little panic. I promise, the other lists won't be as long, I told you this wouldn't be a tasting-notes list and I intend to stick to that. It's also worth noting that for every Mash Gang beer I have drank, there's one I haven't. Their output was insane, which is why in my book, they are the most important players in the game.

Lucky Saint

There are certain names in the alcohol-free beer world that carry a bit of reverence. Like the monks of old who brewed in silence but drank with purpose, these names stand tall amongst fermentation tanks. Perhaps no name is holier, by branding at least, than Lucky Saint.

Launched in 2018 by Luke Boase, at a time when alcohol-free beer options were limited to say the least. Boase didn't come from a brewing dynasty. Instead, he was just another drinker who got tired of having to make the choice between the booze or the bland. After trying a number of alcohol-free beers and not finding one that scratched the itch, he decided to take the long route: He raised some money, knocked on brewery doors across Europe, and found a partner in a Benedictine brewery in Bavaria. Yes, actual monks, you couldn't make it up.

The result? A 0.5% **Unfiltered Lager** with all the depth, body, and crispness you'd expect from the real deal.

Let's be clear, this wasn't an overnight success. Lucky Saint spent over two years developing their flagship beer, but it paid off. The lager quickly became a go-to for pubs, restaurants, supermarkets, and hospitality venues across the UK, and it is now one of the most recognisable alcohol-free brands in Britain. In 2020, Lucky Saint launched on draught. This was the eureka moment the world had been waiting for. Finally, we could go to a pub and have a decent pint. This wasn't a 'lite' beer for people who had given up; it was just a beer.

In 2023, Lucky Saint opened its own pub, The Lucky Saint on Devonshire Street, London. If you're picturing a dry, wellness bar at this point, think again. This place is lively. It's welcoming. It's got alcohol-free pints on draught. It even serves full-strength beers because, in true Lucky Saint style, it isn't preachy. It just gives people options. And frankly, that's all we're after, isn't it?

For years, Lucky Saint stuck with just one beer. One. No grapefruit sours, no imperial stout for dry January dabblers. Just the lager. It was a bold move, it was a clever move. By focusing on one style, they perfected it. Just as 'Carling is lager', Lucky Saint, to most, was alcohol-free lager.

Eventually, they did branch out, releasing a **Hazy IPA** in 2023 and a **Lemon Lager** in 2025.

There are lots of brilliant alcohol-free brewers doing incredible work, but Lucky Saint deserves its flowers. Because, for a lot of us, it was the beer that made us say wait, this can actually be good? Sometimes, that's all you need to change your drinking life forever.

Nirvana Brewery

In the world of alcohol-free beer, some names shout, others whisper.

Nirvana Brewery, tucked away in East London, does neither. It brews, quietly, consistently and with purpose. No gimmicks, just beer.

Founded in 2016, Nirvana was the UK's first dedicated alcohol-free brewery. At a time when most people still thought alcohol-free beer meant watery lager in a dusty corner of a supermarket, Nirvana decided to take it seriously. They brewed it like it mattered, because it did.

It began, as so many of these origin stories do (apart from Mash Gang's crazy fermentation experiments) with a simple problem: Man stops drinking and can't find anything decent to replace beer with. The solution? His sister-in-law, Becky Kean. They founded Nirvana together. I'm not sure if your in-laws have done anything nice for you lately, but I'm fairly sure launching a brewery is a bit of a flex.

Becky has been at the helm ever since, steering the brewery through years of AF evolution, from a fringe moment to a cultural shift. Nirvana endures. The best part? The beers have been getting better and better.

Here are the Nirvana beers I have sampled to date:

Lager: The first Nirvana beer I had was a simple lager. It did everything you would want a lager to do.

Organic Pale Ale: Mid-gold in colour, fairly clean with light caramel and orange.

Pils: An improved lager, less malt-heavy than the initial lager I tried.

Bavarian Helles Lager: This was the first Nirvana beer that really turned my head. The previous beers of theirs I had tried were good, don't get me wrong, but this one is excellent. In a wonderful long-pour bottle, with beautiful biscuit notes. It would stand against any alcohol-free lager.

Cloudy Lemon Lager: Another long-pour bottle, this one is wonderfully balanced, not overly sweet, with the lemon cutting through just enough.

Traditional Bavarian Heifeweizen: A fresh, light, easy-drinking wheat beer. This had just enough spice with a hint of vanilla and banana.

Nirvana Best: As a fan of the classic bitter, I've been utterly disappointed countless times when it comes to alcohol-free bitter attempts. Most are overly malt-sweet. This beer is one of the better ones. It has all the malt characteristics you want with a hit of bitterness at the finish to bring it back. A very solid offering.

Milk Stout: This was a limited batch. Smooth, creamy, delicious.

Nitro Stout: What the name suggests, a nitro stout. It's a fairly solid offering, but I must admit I have had better.

IPA: Solid fridge filler.

Blossom: A Hazy Pale Ale, with a touch of sweetness.

What sets Nirvana apart isn't just what they brew, it's how. Unlike many AF brands that outsource their production, Nirvana does everything on their own East London brewery.

Drop Bear Beer Co

Founded in 2019 by Joelle Drummond and Sarah McNena, Drop Bear became one of the first alcohol-free breweries in the UK to lean into craft identity; flavour first, unapologetically modern and 100% independent. Their brews have included:

New World Lager: Here's the first example in this little list of a beer that says it all in the title. It's a New World Lager. For beers like this going forward, we'll let the name speak for itself. Look at me making the rules up as I go.

Yuzu Pale Ale.

Tropical IPA.

Bonfire Stout: A stout with a smoky malt characteristic.

True Colours: Limited edition IPA for Pride. Juicy, fruity with notes of pineapple, mango and passionfruit.

Drop Bear's range is small, but mighty. Designed to hit the big flavour profiles that drinkers love without the need for alcohol.

Jump Ship Brewing

Ah look, another brewery born out of frustration. Better yet, another female founder. We love to see it. Jump Ship Brewing was founded in 2019 by Sonja Mitchell, a self-described beer lover and mum of three who realised that alcohol wasn't doing her any favours. So, in a move that's half madness, half brilliant, she left her career in marketing and set out to form Scotland's first ever alcohol-free brewery, quite literally jumping ship.

Jump Ship's beers are proudly brewed in Scotland, but the spirit of the brand is thoroughly nautical. The branding is subtle but striking. Sleek cans, seafaring names, and an identity that says that this is for adventurers who like to keep their heads clear. And the beers? Well, here are a few I've had:

Yardarm: Lager.

Jackstaff: IPA.

Flying Colours: Pale.

Stoker's: Stout.

Stoker's Extra Smooth: Nitro Stout.

Dazzle Ship: Galaxy IPA.

Haar: New England IPA.

Ocean Drift: Gooseberry Gose. I have to talk about this one a little. It was the first Jump Ship beer that really turned my head. The others are very solid fridge staples, but the complexity of this beer was wonderful. Perfectly balanced, it hit every single note. From the tart Scottish gooseberries to the touch of salt that brought it all together. It really was a wonderful beer.

Ocean Drift: Yes, another one. In my opinion, this has been the finest beer to leave Scotland. This is a bramble sour. If Jump Ship decided they wanted to go and do sour beer full-time, they could absolutely do that. It's a masterclass in a can.

Uncharted (collab with Pilot): Raspberry and vanilla sour.

What makes Jump Ship feel different is how personal it is. This isn't a big, faceless company trying to ride the sober wave; it's one woman's passion project, backed by a growing crew of beer enthusiasts who believe in it. The authenticity of the brand strikes a chord. They are excellent people, making excellent beer.

We Can Be Friends

Where do I even begin? We Can Be Friends launched in 2023, seemingly from nowhere. Founded by Sam Ray, who was a professional brewer before founding We Can Be Friends, the brand suddenly appeared on social media, releasing their first brew in November of that year.

Sam reached out to me and asked if he could send me a can to try, and I'll be honest, I was apprehensive. I knew nothing of the brand, nor could I find any information online. There have been so many brands come and go in this sphere, often with one subpar liquid, trying to get themselves a little slice of the pie. I thought this could perhaps be another one of those cases.

I could not have been more wrong.

Every single beer that has been released by We Can Be Friends has been nothing short of sensational. For consistency, they are the number one alcohol-free brand in my opinion. They are yet to miss the mark. Releasing beers that have made even the most passionate craft beer lover turn their head and embrace the world of alcohol-free beer.

Their releases to date have been:

Super Liquid: I could really save time here by just writing 'banger' after each beer. Super Liquid was the first release from We Can Be Friends, and it was just that. A banger. Sam primarily makes IPAs because that's what he likes to drink. Which I respect. This one was vibrant, tropical, and floral.

Hypersonic: New England IPA. Soft, pillowy with big, bold notes of pineapple and grapefruit.

Ultraviolet: Pale Ale. Deliciously creamy with an oat-heavy base. A little dank hit of Strata T90 balances out the Citra.

All Night (collab with Track): Bright, zesty IPA with lemon and lime notes.

Substitute (collab with Overtone): Hazy Pale Ale. Smooth, velvety and sweet.

Albino Pasta (collab with Deya): IPA with New Zealand hops, Luminosa and Strata. A big, creamy, lemon and lime-vibe beer.

Turbo Wave: A big, bold IPA, hopped with Citra.

Particles (collab with Overtone): Pale Ale. Fruity and (you guessed it), full-bodied. Honestly, if anybody is ever trying to tell you alcohol-free beer is too thin, give them a We Can Be Friends beer.

Flwrs (collab with Beak): A beer we had all been waiting for. Beak finally entered the alcohol-free world with this sensational collab. A hazy, juicy IPA.

Cloudy Krush (collab with Vault City): A lemon sour beer. Picking up where Mash Gang left off with the Vault City collab range.

A Way With Worlds (collab with Gravity Well): IPA. Juicy and intense.

Sunburst (collab with Sober Boozers Club): Well, well, well. Even typing this feels a little unreal. Sunburst was the first ever collaboration between an alcohol-free brewery and an alcohol-free beer social media commentator (pretty niche, but I'll take it). We were proud of this one, and it was very well received. Of course, I had no doubt it would be because, as stated, all We Can Be Friends beers are excellent. This one had a fluffy base loaded with Motueka T90, Motueka Cryo, Nelson Sauvin, and Citra. Big hits of lime, gooseberries, and tropical delights.

White Light: Dank, resinous IPA.

Heavyweight: A big, bold IPA, zesty and citrusy with a touch of pine.

Phaser (collab with Overtone): Their third collaboration with Overtone, this one has a little mango and melon to complement the sharp grapefruit top notes.

Since their launch, We Can Be Friends have undoubtedly gone on to be amongst the best producers of alcohol-free beer not only in the UK but in the world.

Big Drop

Possibly the first alcohol-free exclusive brewery I had heard of when I was still a drinker of the booze. Big Drop was founded in 2016 by Rob Fink and James Kindred. They were also frustrated with the lack of options available in the alcohol-free beer world. Seems to be a recurring theme in the mid-2010s, doesn't it?

Back in 2016, the idea of good alcohol-free beer was still a little radical, but, alongside Nirvana, Big Drop saw something others didn't. They brought in some of the best brewing minds and took on the challenge like scientists with a hop obsession. The result? A brewery that changed the game.

Big Drop don't remove alcohol from regular beer. Instead, they developed a brewing method that naturally results in beer at 0.5% or less. This was a big deal back in 2016. Today, their beers can be found worldwide. They have won over 100 international beer awards and have helped move alcohol-free beer out of the shadows and into the mainstream spotlight.

Some of their beers include:

Uptime: Craft Lager.

Wildtrack: American Pale Ale.

Waterslide: IPA.

Kodama: IPL. This was a fusion beer utilising the Japanese hop Sorachi Ace alongside Nelson Sauvin, blending citrus and gooseberry notes.

Fieldhopper: Golden Ale.

L'il IPL (collab with Salt): India pale lager.

Rush Rider (collab with Amundsen): Pastry sour.

Woodcutter: Brown ale.

Poolside: DDH IPA.

Coba Maya: Cerveza - Mexican-style lager, or lawnmower beer. It literally translates to 'beer' in Spanish.

Reef Point: Craft lager.

Galactic: Milk stout.

Pine Trail: Pale ale.

Paradiso: Citra IPA.

Big Drop were one of the sparks. A proof of concept. A brewery that showed the world that alcohol-free beer didn't have to be an act of compromise. It could be joyful. It could be bold. It could be craft.

Below Brew Co

One of the first breweries I fell in love with. And, one of the first breweries that made me realise I could still drink all of the beers I used to love without alcohol. Formerly known as Lowtide, Below Brew Co are the kind of brewery that make you do a double take. Not just because the beers taste great (they do), but because the artwork, the names and the culture scream full-strength craft, even though the ABV doesn't break 0.5%.

They have built a brand that doesn't just sit alongside the best alcohol-free outfits, but one that feels like it belongs on the shelves next to Verdant, Northern Monk or Deya. That's no accident, Below Brew Co doesn't aim to be 'good for non-alcoholic beer', they want to be your favourite brewery - full stop.

Some of the Below Brew Co beers I have sampled:

Brune DMC: Belgian-style Brown Ale.

West Coast Hop Lock: Pale Ale.

Forgot To Take My Pils: Hoppy Pilsner.

Promises I Made Myself (collab with Newtown Park): IPA.

NEIPA The Cosmic Turtle: NEIPA with Citra, Amarillo, El Dorado and Mosaic. Tropical and hazy.

Wild Juice Chase: DDH Pale Ale.

Double Dip (collab with Attic Brew Co): Superdelic, Nectaron and Nelson Sauvin come together to create a wonderfully balanced New Zealand IPA.

Unruly AF (collab with Electric Bear): Pale Ale with subtle notes of peach iced tea.

Check This Stout: Pastry Stout.

Ohana (collab with Exhale): Double Dry Hopped pale ale. Big tropical flavours.

Heaven And Helles: Helles-style lager.

Tweet And Sour: Fruit smoothie sour.

All Hopped Up: IPA with flavours of grapefruit, mango, papaya with a piney finish.

Elephant In The Room: Coconut and peach notes make for a piña colada-like pale ale.

Below Brew Co isn't here to talk about wellness. They're not trying to turn beer into a health product. They're here for the beer. That's what makes them so important in the alcohol-free space, because let's be honest, sometimes you want a beer that feels like it was made by beer lovers, not brand strategists. Below Brew Co isn't trying to sell you a new lifestyle, they're simply offering you an option.

BRULO

BRULO was founded in 2019 by James Brown with a mission to raise the standard of alcohol-free beer and to make it widely available. They also happen to be the world's first Bitcoin Treasury Brewery, essentially meaning all of their net profits are reinvested into Bitcoin.

From day one, BRULO have pushed boundaries. They have landed in supermarkets and released some limited-edition beers that have been absolute game-changers:

Lust For Life: BRULO's flagship beer. An IPA double dry-hopped with Citra, Simcoe, and Mosaic.

7 Hop 7 Grain: Double Dry-Hopped IPA.

Highway To Hell: Lager.

5 Fruit Gose: Gose with mango, passionfruit, guava, apricot, and orange.

Sabro Galaxy: IPA.

King For A Day: NEIPA.

Cascadian Tides: Stout.

Big Dream: IPA.

CBD IPA: I said these lists would have no particular order to them. I lied. I put this beer last because for me it is the finest beer BRULO have ever put out into the world. Each can contained 35mg CBD. I'm not particularly fond of 'functional beer', with biotics, etc. I can see the appeal, but when I want a beer, I just want to enjoy the liquid. This beer was the exception to the rule. It also happened to be delicious. Dry-hopped to perfection with delicious notes of pineapple, citrus, and stone fruit, mixed with the dank profile of the CBD, it did everything I could have ever wanted.

BRULO beers are consistently good. If I ever see one in the fridge of a hospitality venue, I know I'm in good hands.

Those are my 'big hitters' if you like. The alcohol-free exclusive breweries that have really impacted me. There are more, that we will go into now, in less detail. This doesn't mean they are inferior, of course; any brewery can produce a beer that is out of this world. I just know how expensive paper is, and if I write essays about every brewery, that will probably cost a lot of money.

Fierce Mild

Would it be a stretch to call Fierce Mild Ireland's answer to Lucky Saint? Probably, but I'm going to do it anyway. They are an alcohol-free brewery based in (you guessed it) Ireland, with one beer to their name currently, the **Fierce Mild Extra Pale Ale**. I have only been able to drink this beer once (multiple bottles in one sitting, mind you), and it was phenomenal. If this beer were available in the UK, it would be in my top five go-to everyday beers.

Clean Break

Founded by Richard Casement on the back of his sobriety, Clean Break launched **Progression**, a pale ale. It was a perfectly sessionable IPA that actually stood up very well against supermarket brews. The company has since transitioned to focus on coaching and supporting people in recovery from addiction.

UNLTD

UNLTD was founded in 2020 by Johnny Johnson, following a break from alcohol. With an incredibly sleek bottle design, they turned my head in my early days of sobriety and were one of the first breweries I discovered. They offer a **lager** and an **IPA**. In 2022, the lager won a European Beer Challenge award.

Days Brewing Co

Available in many UK supermarkets, Days Brewing Co. were founded in 2020 by Mike Gammell and Duncan Keith. I have tried their **lager** and their **pale ale**. Whilst it is impossible to argue Days have impacted the alcohol-free space, with an ever-growing presence, I don't particularly enjoy the liquid. For me, it is too malt-sweet. This is a risk with beer at 0.0% ABV; you can find yourself drinking something that is essentially a malt drink (remember the simulated fermentation method from earlier).

Good Karma Beer Co.

I have not drank enough beer from Good Karma. I'll admit it. I can't tell you why; I just haven't. Yet, every single beer of theirs I have tried has been fantastic. Founded by Steve Sailopal, who was also a co founder of Nirvana, they focus on sustainable brewing practices, using only British malts and hops. The beers I have sampled include:

Positive Vibrations: New England pale ale.

Dhamra: Black IPA.

Sattva: IPA using East Kent Golding Hops.

Chakra: Pale ale.

Tantra: IPA.

Mantra: Lager.

They have released so many more, from sours to special collab brews. Their branding is wonderful, their beer is wonderful, their ethos is wonderful.

Clausthaler

Before people like me were talking about alcohol-free beers that had names like 'Hoptimus Prime', there was Clausthaler in Germany.

The godfather, the original, the alcohol-free beer that was making it work long before it was cool, or even mildly socially acceptable.

If alcohol-free beer today is a thriving, experimental house party, Clausthaler is the silent legend in the corner, sipping their brew and nodding "I was doing this before you were born".

Let's rewind. It's 1970s West Germany. The Berlin Wall is very much still up and alcohol-free beer tasted like watered-down regret. Enter the Binding Brauerei, a Frankfurt-based brewery with a wild idea: What if alcohol-free beer didn't have to be awful?

In 1979, after years of experimenting (and by that I literally mean they invented Controlled Fermentation), they launched Clausthaler, the first beer to be brewed using this exact method. Better yet, they did this in full compliance with the German Reinheitsgebot; the 500-year-old beer purity law that exists in Germany. In short, Clausthaler was the first alcohol-free beer with serious brewing integrity. They are still going strong today.

A few of their core offerings:

Clausthaler Original: Malty, smooth, slightly bitter. German-style lager.

Clausthaler Dry Hopped: A more modern spin, with a little floral edge.

Clausthaler Unfiltered: Cloudy, wheaty, slightly spicy.

Clausthaler Grapefruit: Like a grapefruit radler.

There's a temptation in the alcohol-free world to pretend that everything started in 2019, but Clausthaler was winning international awards for alcohol-free brewing whilst some of us were still in nappies. They were brewing proper 0.5% beer before most of today's breweries even existed, before the internet existed for that matter.

While they don't always get the love they deserve from the craft crowd (guilty), their impact is massive. Without Clausthaler, there's a chance we'd still be sipping on sugary malt water and pretending we like it. I'll be honest. Clausthaler isn't the beer I reach for regularly, but it is a beer I respect. It's like the original Obi-Wan vs Vader fight, perhaps a little dated but undeniably iconic.

Fungtn

A brewery about as far removed from Clausthaler as it's possible to be. Founded by Zoey Henderson in 2020, Fungtn produced a range of alcohol-free beers brewed with micro-adaptogens, or medicinal mushrooms. The company unfortunately stopped trading in 2024.

The beers they offered included:

Chaga Lager.

Reishi Citra Beer.

Lions Maine IPA.

Shiitake Dark Lager.

These guys were one of the first of their kind, making use of adaptogens in alcohol-free beer. Whilst I have stated adaptogen beer doesn't particularly sing to me, the liquid itself was actually decent.

Athletic Brewing Co

If I were an American gentleman, Athletic Brewing Co would have likely featured much higher on this list. Over there, it's the stuff of legend, an alcohol-free juggernaut. In the UK? It's a supermarket beer, a relatively poor one at that. This frustrates me to no end, because some of the beers Athletic put out in America sound incredible, they just don't let us Brits have them. However, on the off chance you ever find yourself presented with a can of the real American stuff, let's break them down a little.

Athletic Brewing Co was founded in 2017 by Bill Shufelt, a hedge fund manager who gave up alcohol for health reasons, and John Walker, a seasoned brewer. Their beer is brewed from scratch to stay under 0.5%, avoiding the dealcoholization process. This landed very well with American drinkers.

Athletic went from indie upstart to multi-million-dollar powerhouse in a few short years. In the US, their beers are everywhere. They've raised tens of millions of dollars in funding, built enormous brewing facilities, and churn out more beer than most British breweries could dream of (but we can't have any good stuff, remember that). In America, for most, Athletic is a staple in the world of alcohol-free beer.

So what on earth happened to Athletic in the UK? In short, they send us their most basic beer:

Upside Dawn: IPA.

Run Wild: Golden ale.

Now, these beers are by no means terrible; they're just not very exciting. Honestly, have a look at some of the brews they put out in

America; it's not fair. However, being me, I have managed to source just one American Athletic Brewing Co. beer in my time. It was a **black IPA**, and it was so. Darn. Good. If anything, I wish I had never drank it because it made me even more angry.

While we're on the topic of American beer I can't drink, there are multiple breweries I see regular updates from that are well and truly on my bucket list for the next time I visit the USA. Some American brews I have been fortunate to be able to import, however, these are just a few (of the many) breweries that have eluded me:

Go Brewing

Best Day Brewing

Good Time Brewing

Roaming Nobles

Drink Sip

Busty Lush

Capacity Brewing

Runners High Brewing Co

Bravus Brewing Company

Atmos Brewing Co

I'm not going to go into any more detail than that because I'll be angry all evening if I do. But you should absolutely check them out if you're on that side of the Atlantic any time soon.

Bero

Actually, I do have a little more to say about American breweries.

Bero launched in 2024. Founded by Tom Holland (yes, the actual Spiderman), they offered three core beers. The **Kingston Golden Pils,** the **Edge Hill Hazy IPA,** and the **Noon Wheat**. The branding was slick, the brand story was one I could get behind, with Tom being so open about his own sober journey, and the liquid looked good. Then they launched. Guess what? It was only available in America. This has since been rectified, and the beer is actually rather good. They have gone on to release another beer, it's an IPA called **Double Tasty;** as of writing, I am yet to try this one. Anyway, Bero beer is good, even if they did tease us Brits for a while.

Smashed Drynks

Founded in 2017 by Richard Clark, Smashed Drynks had the first purpose-built cool vacuum distillation plant in the UK. This essentially means that they can produce full alcohol liquids and then remove the alcohol. They have a fairly basic range of beers, including a **lager**, a **citrus beer,** and a **pale ale**.

Infinite Session

Also founded in 2017 (popular year), in Hackney Wick, Infinite Session have cracked UK supermarkets with a very solid IPA. They have released some limited-edition beers, but their core item is the **Infinite Session IPA**.

Impossibrew

We're finishing on four 'mood-enhancing' beer brands. The most known is probably Impossibrew (did you know they were on Dragons' Den?). Impossibrew essentially offers beers that they claim will enhance your natural alpha brain waves, promoting relaxation. They use a whole load of ingredients like Ashwagandha and L-Theanine as well as their own alcohol-alternative formula. I have, of course, tried their beers and I actually did feel a very mild buzz. Almost like I'd had a little too much coffee. It could have been placebo, it could have been science, I wouldn't claim to be an expert on such things. I'm just here to tell you these beers exist. They have a **lager**, a **pale ale** and they once did a collab beer with Mash Gang called **Red Alert**, which was a red ale.

NuWave

Fairly new on the scene, NuWave also offers beers that claim to give the drinker a nice 'two-pint buzz', using adaptogens and botanicals. They currently offer a **lager** and a **hazy pale ale**.

Exhale Nutrition

You guessed it, another company with a range of beers claiming to offer more than just taste. Exhale Nutrition have picked up where Fungtn left off, with two beers making use of medicinal mushrooms. They have a **Reishi Stout** and a **Lion's Mane IPA**.

Collider

Alcohol-free beer infused with mushrooms and botanicals. They aim to relax you without alcohol. Their range currently consists of a **lager** and a **Session IPA**.

NOLIA

I said we were finished - I lied. In June 2025 (the day after I finished this list that had already taken me much longer to complete than anticipated (cheers guys), the people from Beak Brewery launched NOLIA. In their words, NOLIA is an alcohol-free brewing project, with a mission to create alcohol-free beer that looks, smells and tastes like a top-tier IPA. They launched as a separate brand to Beak as they did not want to dilute the brand they already had. Their aim for NOLIA is to create the UK's best premium alcohol-free IPA. Which is no small task.

There will naturally be more alcohol-free exclusive breweries out there. As stated previously, there are new companies popping up all the time; such is the appeal of alcohol-free beer in the modern world. This is a small sample of a much larger world, but I think if you stuck to these breweries for the rest of your life, you wouldn't go far wrong.

Supermarket Beers

The wild west. For every fantastic supermarket brew, there is a terrible one. Supermarkets are a scary place for the early non-drinker. They offer comfort in familiarity, with known brands beckoning from the shelf, but beware. Many have never returned to the no and low section after their first dance with such liquids.

They're hit and miss, is what I'm saying. However, when a good supermarket beer drops, it really is handy.

I won't go into detail on each brand; chances are you'll know them, but I'll give you a quick verdict on each.

St Austell: Proper Job: A fantastic beer. Truly fantastic. I have not actually met anybody with anything negative to say about this one (yet).

Guinness 0: Arguably the most important alcohol-free beer in the market. Guinness spent a lot of money on their alcohol-free stout, and it worked. Virtually indistinguishable from the full alcohol version (I still find it a little sweet), Guinness gave full alcohol drinkers the nod of approval to try alcohol-free beer. If Guinness tells you it's okay to drink, chances are it is. If you ever want to strike up a positive conversation about alcohol-free beer with somebody, ask them if they've tried the Guinness.

Heineken: The single most dangerous drink in the world (remember, my opinion only). There are people out there who will have tried an alcohol-free beer for the first time and ruled the entire operation off due to Heineken 0. I don't even fall into the group of people who disliked the alcoholic version; it was actually a go-to lager of mine. This stuff though, awful. Worse than Becks Blue.

Budweiser: The first time I tried an alcohol-free Budweiser, I thought it was pretty rubbish. The second time, I was pleasantly surprised. It's not a drink I buy out of choice, but if it's at a function I'll gladly enjoy it.

Madri: If you like your beer to taste like metal, this one is for you.

Birra Morretti: Don't do it to yourself.

Stella Artois: The best of the macro lagers in my opinion. It actually tastes like Stella. I actually reached for a bottle of Stella quite often in early sobriety, which is a fact I'm only just remembering now. Worth a try in my opinion.

Carlsberg: OK, so there's a little bit to break down with Carlsberg, so bear with me here…

Carlsberg have an alcohol-free beer available in the UK. It's dreadful. Truly dreadful. However, Carlsberg also offers different alcohol-free beers in other parts of the world. They have a **hoppy lager**, they have **Carlsberg Nordic**, and they have **Carlsberg**

Danish Pilsner. All of these beers are actually very good. They even launched a project brewing alcohol free beers that were made using 100% renewable energy, that would be shipped by electric freight transport using AI-powered technology. I wrote to Carlsberg (over sixty times, I'm not even joking, they shouted at me in the end) asking them to stock these beers in the UK, which they refuse to do. I got other people to write to Carlsberg (again, they got quite upset with me), who were met with the same response. So, if you're not in the UK for whatever reason, give Carlsberg a try. If you are, don't.

Peroni: Average at best.

Becks Blue: Well, what can I say? I actually think Becks Blue gets a little too much stick. It is bad, don't get me wrong, but I've certainly had worse. I can just about manage two bottles of it before I have to stop.

Chouffe Alcohol Free: Pretty darn good.

Leffe: A little sweet for me.

Hoegarden: Again, slightly too sweet.

Erdinger: I don't actually mind this. I'll get it if I'm in a chain pub (you know the one). They did release a **grapefruit** version, which I rather enjoyed also.

Brooklyn Special Effects: Pretty top-tier.

Free Damm: My go-to supermarket lager. It's crisp and completely smashable. You can also get it on tap in some locations, which is lovely.

Corona: Pretty good. It got me through my first sober wedding, so I'll always be grateful to Corona for that.

Doom Bar: I dislike this. A lot.

Rheinbacker Pilsner: Awful.

Estrella Galicia: Pretty decent.

Asahi: I don't mind the Asahi 0 we get over here in the UK.

However, I was lucky enough to sample an Asahi brew that was sent to me from Japan. It was called **Beery**, and it's one of the best lagers I have ever drank. Again, a case of the UK not being allowed nice things.

Adnams Ghost Ship: I don't get on with this one, but others swear by it.

Bitburger: Pretty middle of the road. They also released a Lemon Radler, which was actually okay.

Tennants: I found this in a supermarket in Scotland. I was disappointed.

Beavertown Lazer Crush: It's not bad, it's not amazing.

Northern Monk Holy Faith: If this were more consistent, it would be a real contender for best supermarket beer. If you get a good can, it's incredible. If you get a bad can, it's pretty average.

Thornbridge Green Mountain: Another case of the cursed large-batch supermarket alcohol-free brew (that's a mouthful). When this beer is good, it's excellent. When it's not, it's not.

Kronenbourg 1664 Biere: I really enjoy this. It's a lovely, delicate lager.

San Miguel: If it's really, really cold, it's not bad, I guess.

Kirkstall Virtuous: This could be really, really good, it's just a little (I hate to say this) thin.

St Peter's Without: There are a few beers in this range. They are all bad.

Perlenbacher Pils: Terrible.

Brewdog: They have a few alcohol-free beers. The only one really worth trying is **Wingman**. That's all I'll say about Brewdog.

Theakston: Nowt Peculier: Brewed using the original recipe of Old Peculier, Theakston dropped this bombshell on us. It's complex, it's rich. It is a little malt-heavy, but my goodness, it's close to the original.

M&S Range: M&S have done something interesting here. They have produced a range of own-brand alcohol-free beers with various breweries. They have a **peach pale ale** brewed with Renegade, a **craft lager** brewed with Hepworth, a **pale ale** with Adnams, and a **Czech lager** with Litovel. They all taste identical to said breweries' beers.

Other Macro Beers With An Alcohol-Free Offering

These aren't supermarket beers per se, but it felt wrong putting them into the beers in the wild section. Don't ask me why, it's my list so it's my rules, okay?

Kingfisher: Average.

Coors Edge: Pretty good, though this was shipped to me from America.

Bud Lime: Fantastic.

Cobra: Bad.

Bavaria: Very bad.

Amstel: Decent.

Mythos: Also fairly decent.

Desperados: Kind of weird.

Jupiler: Not for me.

Skol: No thanks.

Staropramen: Double no thanks.

Veltins: Triple no thanks (there's a theme here).

Stiegel: More or less okay.

And there we have, more or less, your supermarket beers (and other macros, MY LIST). There are, of course, new lines being added all the time, so chances are the day after you read this there will be a big launch that Ben didn't mention, but I can't see the future, so this will have to do. What I hope it does highlight is the range of alcohol-free beer that is actually available. You can also take this list further; if you venture into Europe, you'll find tostadas and lemon variants of these beers (a few have snuck their way into the UK already, so keep an eye out).

We've covered alcohol-free breweries, we've covered supermarkets, and I'm seeing a whole load of beers. Almost too many, you could say (if you were the one writing this list out and wondering why you didn't make actual tasting notes whilst you drank the beers the first time around).

However, if you thought this list of beer was enough to get on with, you're wrong. Remember the wild beers? The one-off releases, the releases to complement their alcoholic counterparts, the releases from breweries across the world? We haven't even started on those beers.

Beers In The Wild

Whilst we will be mentioning some fantastic UK breweries here, I need to give a little nod to a company called Onder Nul Punt Vijf, or ONP5. They are based in the Netherlands and they sell a lot of fabulous European beer. I have been able to source some of the best beer I have ever drank from all over the world thanks to these guys, beers that I would otherwise have not been able to try.

So, beers in the wild? This will be primarily list-based, with a few comments thrown in if I see fit. Again, some of these beers will no longer be available; it's mostly for me to show how many alcohol-free beers the world has to offer (and to show my mum that I actually am doing something in my spare time now I'm not drinking booze). The first breweries we will list have released multiple alcohol-free beers that I have tried.

Sheep in Wolf's Clothing

Some of the first alcohol-free beers I tried when getting sober came from Sheep in Wolf's Clothing. I had their **Easy Rinder**, which was a wheat beer, their **Lager Day Saints**, which was a lager (obviously), and their **Small Kingdom IPA**. They were really good beers. You don't see their alcohol-free beers around all that often anymore, which is a shame. I managed to find a can of Lager Day Saints recently, and it held up very, very well all these years later.

Northern Monk

One of the most beloved breweries in the UK, for a reason. Northern Monk has put out some fantastic alcohol-free beers over the years, in addition to their supermarket offering. We have had their **Mango Lassie Heathen, Bruce** (a chocolate cake stout collaboration with indie bakery Get Baked), **The Pilgrimage**, which was a part of their Patrons Projects series, **Great Northern Lager, Heaven**, a chocolate and maple stout, **Peak**, which was a lager, and **Holy Heathen**, which was one of the best New England IPAs you could ever wish to drink.

Thornbridge

Alongside Green Mountain, Thornbridge had previously released **Zero Five**, a pale ale. They most recently released an alcohol-free version of their famous beer **Jaipur**.

Lervig

The Lervig **No Worries** series are great beers. They come in a variety of flavours, such as **grapefruit, pineapple, mango**, and **lemon**. They have also released limited-batch versions such as their **No Worries Driving Home for Christmas**, which was a dark ale.

Cloudwater

For a brewery that doesn't only focus on alcohol-free beer, Cloudwater boasts an impressive collection. By this, I mean, they have all been fantastic. The first alcohol-free Cloudwater beer I drank was **Fresh**, an incredible IPA. They also released a Citra edition of this. From that point, they have released a number of collab and limited-edition beers such as **Cheeky Vimno** (a sour, based on what you're imagining), **Boring AF**, which was a hibiscus sour they made with Manchester-based Dry Bar Love From (they have sadly since closed shop). Carrying on with the sours, they released a **Pink Grapefruit Radler**, a **Negroni Sour,** and a **Margarita Gose**. They then released a collab beer with Manchester-based musician Luke Una called **Everything Above the Sky**. For their ten-year anniversary, Cloudwater released a collection of beers to celebrate, including an alcohol-free beer. This beer was called **Repose**. It was an IPA and may just be their best alcohol-free beer to date.

Funky Fluid

There are two sides to Funky Fluid's alcohol-free beer range, both as wonderful as the other. On one hand, they offer their **Free Gelato** range of sour beers. With wonderful flavour combinations such as Berries and Cream, Mango and Sticky Rice, Tropical Punch and Tropical Smoothie. On the other hand, they prove they have more than one string to their bow, with some fantastic beers such as **Coffee Point Five**, which is a New England IPA brewed with specialty coffee from HAYB, and **Free Cloudy,** which is a New England IPA.

Tiny Rebel

Tiny Rebel's alcohol-free range includes an alcohol-free version of **Clwb Tropica**, **Space Cake** (stout), and **Speak Easy**, which was a collaboration brew with So Let's Talk.

Birmingham Brewing Company

One of my local breweries. They make fantastic beer (I can vouch for the alcoholic beer they make too from my drinking days, though I shouldn't). They currently have two alcohol-free brews on offer: We have the **Sober Brummie IPA** and the **Sober Brummie Stout**.

Omnipollo

Swedish masters Omnipollo have created some of the most head-turning brews with their **Bianca** series. In particular, their Lassi Gose beers, with a head so dense it will actually rise above the rim of your glass. In the Lassi Gose range, we have had a **blueberry maple pancake**, a **raspberry peach marshmallow,** a **blackberry marshmallow,** and a brew called **Space Jam**, which had blueberries in it. These beers are like no other. They're rich, tart, and intense. They also released a **Pineapple Bianca**, which tasted more like pineapple than some actual pineapples do. They have also released some more 'conventional' beers which have been fantastic. These include **Knox, Fortuna, Eternal Now, Pattern of Play,** and an

Oaked Vintermust Sour, which was their take on the traditional Swedish Christmas drink Julmust.

Mikkeller

The first alcohol-free beer I had from Mikkeller was called **Caraxes**. It was a limited-edition Dragonfruit sour to celebrate the TV series House of the Dragon. They have a regular range of beers similar to this. That range is called **Limbo**. In this range, I have tried a Dragonfruit variant, a Riesling variant, and a Mango variant. Other beers in their range include **Wonder**, a wheat beer, **Drink'in the Sun**, another wheat beer, **Weird Weather**, an IPA, **Easy Peasy**, a New England IPA, and **Drink'in the Snow**, a winter ale.

Only With Love

A fantastic brewery with some fantastic beers in their alcohol-free range. Their **Juicy AF** beers are some of the most delicious on the market. In this range, we have had a **Mango Pale Ale**, a **New Zealand Pale Ale**, and an **American Pale Ale**. They also released **Zippy AF,** a blackcurrant and cherry sour, **Easy AF**, an IPA, and a **Nectaron Mango Hop Soda** in collaboration with Enough.

Arbour Ales

There have been three alcohol-free beers from Arbour: **Wish You Were Beer**, **Baseline** (in collaboration with Ravers 2 Runners), and **New Horizons**.

Ammundsen Brewery

Ammundsen have a pretty wide range of alcohol-free beer. They have the **Eazy Peazy IPA**, the **Razzle Dazzle** pastry sour, the **Eazy Rider** IPA, a classic **Helles**, a **Lemon Radler**, and a series of dessert beers, such as the **Raspberry And Custard Berlinner**, the **Chocolate Chip Cookie Dessert Beer,** and the **Cinnamon S'mores Dessert Beer.** They also released a pretty wild **Electric Mango Bubballoo Sour**. These beers all hold up fairly well, but if they could refine them even slightly, they could be incredible.

Nøgne

Nøgne offer a variety of alcohol-free beers, including their **Himla**

Humla IPA, **Stripped Craft** lime-infused ale, **Tropical IPA,** and a **Milk Stout**.

Renegade

Renegade have offered **Brewski**, a peach beer, and **Solo**, a pale ale.

Brew By Numbers

Their alcohol-free releases have included a **Blood Orange Pale Ale** and a classic **Pale Ale**.

Kasteel

I have sampled two alcohol-free beers from Kasteel: **Kateel Rouge** and **Kasteel Tropical**.

Bohemia Regent

They have released **Renégát,** a Czech-style pilsner, and **Regent Lemon**, a lemon lager.

Unbarred

Brighton-based brewery Unbarred entered the alcohol-free space with **LowKey**, a pale ale. They followed it up with **Coastin'**, a West Coast IPA.

Deya

For years (it felt), I had been waiting for Deya to enter the alcohol-free scene. I had heard rumblings from sources close to the brewery that it absolutely was not on the cards. Then they did. It's a good time to be alive. Alongside their collab beers mentioned previously, they have produced some solo brews such as **Spoken Into Existence** and **Write A To Do List**. They also released another collab brew with Left Handed Giant and Verdant called **Circus Of The Sun**. Alcohol-free beer seems to be a part of Deya's release schedule now, and I am so here for it.

Verdant

Speaking of which, iconic Cornish brew powerhouses Verdant have released some alcohol-free beers in their own right. They dropped a small-batch brew titled **Small Batch 6**, followed by **PSYCH!**, an absolutely massive IPA.

Left Handed Giant

The final brewery in the Deya collab trifecta, Left Handed Giant have released beers such as **Run Free** and **Free Motion**.

Brew York

Brew York already had a pretty solid range of alcohol-free beers such as **Loris** and **Blue Jay**. Then they did something wonderful. They released an alcohol-free version of **Juice Forsyth**. I never got to drink the full alcohol version of this beer, which pained me. What I can say is the alcohol-free version is darn delicious.

Wiper And True

Bristol-based brewery Wiper and True have put a lot of work into their alcohol-free range. They released **Kaleidoscope** (pale ale) and **Tomorrow** (lager), which both went down very well amongst consumers. Then, in January 2025, they did something pretty wild. They released four limited-edition alcohol-free beers, collaborating with a different brewery for each. We had **First Draught**, a pale ale collaboration with Track. Then we had **Double Take**, a fantastic dry stout brewed in collaboration with The Five Points Brewing Co. We had **Third Time's A Charm**, a West Coast IPA with Elusive Brewing, and we had **Four Quarters**, a grapefruit radler brewed with Northern Monk.

Sierra Nevada

Talking about big moments for alcohol-free beer: Sierra Nevada. This was one of my coming-of-age beers as a drinker of beer. The iconic Sierra Nevada Pale Ale. When I gave up alcohol, I accepted the fact that I would never drink a Sierra Nevada beer again. I underestimated the pull of alcohol-free beer. Sierra Nevada has released a number of alcohol-free beers. I have been able to sample two to date. The **Trail Pass IPA** and the **Trail Pass Golden**. There are other alcohol-free brews out there from Sierra Nevada too, I just haven't been able to get my hands on them. The beers themselves are relatively good. No, they don't quite live up to the full alcohol version, but they're close enough.

Insel Brauerei

Alcohol-free beers from Insel Brauerei include **Skippers Pilsner, Surfers Summer Ale, Snorkelers IPA,** and **Snorkelers Sea Salt IPA.**

Õllenaut

Beers from the Õllenaut **Kainken** range (their alcohol-free collection) include an **IPA**, a **Pale Ale,** and a **Smoked Porter.**

VandeStreek Brouwerij

Remember ages ago when I talked about Café Gollem in Amsterdam? These beers really helped me out there. I had already tried their **Hard Pour Coffee Stout**. However, in Amsterdam, I tried **Playground** (IPA), **Fun House** (NEIPA), and I got myself a **Grapefruit IPA** that I drank on the Eurostar on the way home. They were all great beers.

Queer Brewing

Queer and trans-owned and run brewery Queer Brewing makes beer in London. They donate portions of their profits to LGBTQ+ charities, and they are a great bunch of people. They released **Bold**, their first alcohol-free beer, which was pretty good. They went on to re-brew that with a few little tweaks that turned it into a top-tier beer. They have also released **Italic**, which is a very good pale ale.

Tartarus Beers

Based in Leeds, Tartarus Beers brews small-batch craft beer, taking inspiration from all things mythical. The first of their alcohol-free beers I tried was a brew called **Pixie**, a hazy pale ale. This was one of the most hard-hitting beers I had ever tried. If you imagine a strong craft beer, then amplify it. I think this could have passed for an 8% beer in a blind taste test; it was almost too much. They also released **Moon Rabbit**, which was a stout.

Brouwerij 't IJ

A fabulous brewery in Amsterdam, known also as The IJ Brewery.

They are the oldest craft brewery in the Netherlands. Of their range, I have tried their **Vrijwit**, a wheat beer, their IPA, which is simply called **Free IPA**, and a beer called **Berrie**, which was a raspberry sour.

Firebrand Brewing Company

I first drank a Firebrand beer in Cornwall, where they are based, and I loved it. In their alcohol-free range, they have **Little Wave**, which is a lager, and **Shorebreak**, which is a hazy IPA.

Stewart Brewing

Scottish brewery of the year 2024, Stewart Brewing has two alcohol-free options in their range, under the **Scott Free** brand. They have a lager and a pale ale. They're very solid brews.

Silver Rocket Brewing

Silver Rocket currently has two alcohol-free beers available: **Hellesbound** (lager) and **Juice Train** (hazy pale ale).

Cold Bath Brewing Co

Cold Bath Brewing Co initially released **1571**, which is a fantastic pale ale. Following the success of this, they released an alcohol-free **lager**.

Ilkley Brewery

An ever-present figure in the world of alcohol-free beer, Ilkley has a series of alcohol-free beers that have been around for a little while now. We have **Maiden Mary** (pale ale), **Nowt Mary** (milk stout), and **Day Dreamer** (lager).

Theodor Schiøtz Brewing Company

A friend of mine brought me two beers back from a visit to Denmark. They fall under the umbrella of **Anarkist**. The beers in question were a New England IPA and a mild. They were both good brews. The mild wasn't what I wanted it to be. A little citrusy and fairly malt-heavy, but it was a nice take on a classic mild.

Huyghe Brouwerij

If you would have told me in 2022 that I would one day drink Delirium again, I'd have assumed we were discussing a relapse. Until **Delirio** arrived. You heard me, alcohol-free Delirium. It's spicy, it's full-bodied, it's fruity. It's quite literally Delirium, without all that alcohol getting in the way of the actual taste of the beer. These guys have also brought us **Paranoia** (otherwise known as the Hippo Beer) alcohol-free and **Paranoia Rouge**, which is a cherry beer. They ticked off so many things on my bucket list with these three beers (well, they ticked off three things, but they were big things).

Butcombe Brewing Co

There are two alcohol-free beers currently in the Butcombe range. We have **Goram**, an IPA that has won countless awards, and **Tall Tales**, a juicy pale ale.

Primator

I have tried three alcohol-free beers from Primator. We have **Free Mother-in-Law**, which came as a classic beer or as a **Pomelo** (basically, it was fruity). We also have the **Nealko**. All three of these beers hit the spot pretty well.

Maltgarden

I have sampled two alcohol-free beers from Polish brewery Maltgarden. Their **Free Sunset**, which is a fruit ale, and also **Free Sunset Red**, another fruit ale.

Hammerton Brewery

Beers in the Hammerton alcohol-free range include **Zed**, a pale ale, **Muse AF**, another pale ale, **Crunch**, a peanut butter milk stout, and **Fudge City**, a chocolate fudge cake stout.

Track Brewing Co

Track first released their alcohol-free version of **Sonoma**, to mixed reviews. Having not sampled the full alcohol version, I was fairly impressed by this one, but amongst some craft beer lovers, the two didn't quite match up. In my eyes, their real triumph was their second alcohol-free release: **Arosa**. This is a helles lager, and it may well be the finest lager I have drank. I have not had a beer from the UK that comes close to this in terms of standing against a classic Bavarian helles. It's exceptional.

Fierce Beer

Fierce Beer has released a stout called **Noir,** a **Rhubarb IPA** and a delicious **Peach lager.**

And there we have every (I think) brewery who has released multiple alcohol-free beers that have met my lips. Surely we're done? No, we are not. The following breweries have released a single alcohol-free beer (that I have tried; chances are they've released more, but again, I'm just one person).

Earth Ales: Verbs: A pale ale infused with lemon verbena. Earth ales are based in Oxfordshire and release seasonal small batch beers made using natural brewing methods with wild and foraged ingredients. The beer was fantastic.

König Ludwig: Weissbier: A wheat beer.

Menabrea: This belongs in the macro section really in terms of quality. Much better than a Heineken but that isn't saying much.

Bristol Beer Factory: Clear Head: IPA. This is about as reliable a beer as you could wish to find.

Viru: Blanc: I just love the bottle. The beer itself is actually decent too.

Barsham Brewery: Stacked AF: Barshams debut alcohol free beer. The malt characteristics here really blew me away. There was no artificial, synthetic sweetness coming through. Instead you had a wonderful, rich brew with a bitter finish.

Utopian Brewing: AF Pilsner: A bright, floral pilsner.

Pistonhead: Flat Tire: Pretty forgettable.

Pearse Lyons Brewery: Foxes Rock IPA: This actually impressed me. It's not one I'd drink again but it over-performed expectations.

Hogs Back Brewery: Little Swine: Pale ale.

Padstow Brewing Company: Crew Brew: Another classic. With some proceeds going to the Cornwall Air Ambulance.

Mariestads: Påskbrygd: Possibly my favourite beer of all time. Hidden all the way down here. This is a seasonal brew by the Swedish brewery, released for a few weeks a time around easter. It's technically a dark lager, but it has all the characteristics of a mild. I adore this beer.

Flensburger: Radler: As the name suggests, this is a radler. A well balanced one at that.

Birra Mania: Après Bici: A white IPA.

Brauerei Göller: Göller Alkoholfrei: Classic helles.

Ægir Bryggeri: Minus: Pale ale.

Kehrwieder: ü. NN IPA: One of Germany's first alcohol free IPAs.

Samuel Smith's Brewery: Sam's Brown Ale: You may dislike this brewery, but, their alcohol-free offering is undeniably good. A brown ale that again avoids the synthetic malt sweetness trap that so many fall into.

Tempest Brewing Co: Ghost Rider: A very solid, rather fruity pale ale.

Schneider Weisse: Weissbier: One of the best weissbiers you could wish to drink.

Rothaus Tannenzäpfle: Pilsner: Fairly decent. It won't blow you away but it's worth picking one up if you see it in the wild.

Nils Oscar: Kalasöl: A solid lager.

Hawkshead Brewery: Trail Angel: Pale ale.

TeeDawn: Golden Pilz: As you've probably guessed, a lager.

Newbarns Brewery: Nae: Pale ale, very hop forward.

Dugges: Tropic Thunder: A sour fruited ale. Passionfruit and peach are the leading flavours.

Bowness Bay Brewing: Swan Free: American triple hopped IPA.

Gebrouwen door Vrouwen: Bloesem Bluf: The brewery name translates to "Brewed By Women". This was a delicious floral beer with elderflower.

Hitachino Nest Beer: Yuzu Ginger Ale: An absolutely top notch ginger ale.

Jopen: Non: This isn't great, nor is it terrible.

Two Chefs Brewing: Funky Falcon: An inoffensive pale ale with lemongrass.

TOAST Brewing: Changing Tides Lager: TOAST Brewing use surplus bread to brew their beer. Changing Tides Lager is a perfectly smashable lager.

Whiplash: Never Drinking Again: I'm very fond of this beer. A solid IPA.

Lost Pier Brewing: Low Hanging Fruit: An incredibly fruity, tropical number. Candy sweet notes cut through, similar to Rainbow Drops sweets.

Glaca Craft Beers: Holy Roasty: Coffee stout

Attic Brew Co: Lucid: Some of the finest Birmingham juice you'll ever drink (have you ever tried our tap water?).

Hawkstone: Spa Lager: Jeremy Clarkson released an alcohol-free beer. That's funny for some reason. This lager is actually pretty decent, if a little forgettable.

De Kromme Haring: Sand Diver: A light, citrusy beer with a subtle sourness.

Lowlander Beer: 0.00% Wit: Middle of the road.

Harvey's Brewery: Old Ale: This missed the mark, but only just. Far better than most beers of a similar nature.

Budels: Radler: Alcohol-free radlers are usually decent, this was no exception.

Anders Brewery: Good Old Days: I really enjoyed this one.

Farm Yard Brew Co: Easy Sunshine: A very well made pale ale.

Mors Craft Beer: Free IPA: A brewery close to my heart. These guys sent me some beer very early into my journey into the world of alcohol-free beer. I love this beer, it blew me away.

Hofmeister: Ultra Low: Not bad at all.

Sudden Death Brewing Co: Lübi Libre: A lemon lime beer, with the fruit only adding a hint of flavour to an already solid beer. There are other versions of this beer in the range, with different fruit combinations, I'm yet to try those.

Lakedown Brewing Co: Sound: An every day smashable pilsner.

Bellwoods Brewery: Stay Classy: IPA.

Uiltje Brewing Co: Bird Of Prey: Used to be known as "Superb Owl", this is a fruity IPA.

Ocean Beer: A Portugese brand with a focus on ocean conservation. Profits from sales of the beer go towards this mission. The liquid itself itn't the best, I have to be honest with you, but the cause is good so we can forgive that (just this once).

Neon Raptor Brewing Co: Cheat Codes: Neon Raptor's first alcohol-free beer. I had to triple check that. This is delicious.

Gloucester Brewery: Zero Gravity: I buy this beer every time I visit The Cotswolds. That's a rather pointless fact but a fact nonetheless. It's good.

Tap Social Movement: Day Release: Tap social movement are an Oxfordshire based organisation helping to secure work for prisoners on day release and for prison leavers. The liquid itself is also excellent.

Siren Craft Brew: Soundwave: A fantastic beer.

Browar Birbant: Turbo%: Sour.

North Brewing Co: Flat Moon Society: A very decent pale ale.

Frontaal Brewing Company: Juice Punch: New England IPA.

Brugse Zot: Sport Zot: This did everything I wanted it to. A delicious Belgian style beer.

Hert Bier: Go Go Ginger: It feels strange to say, but with the name, I wanted more ginger.

Stormtrooper Beer: Space Race: So, as an alcohol-free beer this one is actually pretty bad. But, it's Star Wars so you know I'm going to buy it every time I see it.

Doing Zero: Hazy Lazy IPA: I very much enjoyed this one.

Ölgerðin Egill Skallagrímsson: Gull: When my friends go on holiday they bring me back beer. I got this one from a supermarket in Iceland (well, my friends did).

Rock City Brewing: Second Date: An acceptable beer to drink.

Locolife: Loco Naranja IPA: Brewed with Spanish oranges. This is a good one.

Brasserie Lefebvre: Ana Hop: A modern Belgian blonde.

Brouwerij de Hoorn BV: Cornet Oaked: There is some serious history to this beer. In the 18th century it would have been brewed in oak barrels. The style was created after a steward of Diepensteyn castle was asked to brew a strong beer. The stewards name? Theodor Cornet. Cornet beer would only be served on special occasions to important guests. Today, oak barrels have been replaced by oak chips in the brewing process to give a full bodied, vanilla taste. The beer is delicious.

Brew Toon: Divernaut: IPA.

La Trappe: Nillis: Another bucket list moment. Drinking a Trappist beer without alcohol? Impossible surely? This beer didn't let me down in the slightest.

Viven Brouwerij: Nada IPA: You guessed it, an IPA.

The Veil Brewing Co: Ever Calm: One of the hardest hitting goses I have ever tried. I had this sent over from America and if all of their sour beer tastes like this, I feel bad for their acid reflux stomachs. Don't get me wrong, it was delicious, but my goodness.

Spaten-Franziskaner-Löwenbräu-Gruppe: Spaten Alkoholfrei: German lager. Real German lager. Inject it into my veins.

Fierce And Noble: Cheers Mind: A light pale ale. Super easy drinking.

Gower Brewery: Gower Zero: IPA.

Bini Brew Co: Rockin' In The Free World: Hazy Pale Ale.

Merakai Brewing Co: Berry Berry Nice: I wanted more from this. The can promised banana, marshmallow, berry and vanilla. I got a whisper of all of them, just not the full flavour slap I wanted.

Campervan Brewery: Off-Piste: I first drank a can of this at Beer X in Liverpool. The can is adorable, the branding is on point, the beer itself is also great. Winner.

Buxton Brewery: Axed: Hop forward beer. Very well made.

Flötzinger Bräu: Hell Alkoholfrei: Another German banger.

Dutch Bargain: Hakuna Batata: These guys use sweet potatoes that have been rejected by shops to make their beer. Which means I like them because food waste is bad. The beer itself was also good. You can actually pick up on the sweet potato and it works. Like beetroot in a chocolate cake.

Labietis: Skaidrais Mežs: Juniper berry infused beer. Very tasty.

Dok Brewing Company: Dokkie: A sour beer.

Cölner Hofbräu Früh: Kölsch: Fairly standard. Another beer that falls into the 'mostly fine' category.

Browar Zakładowy: Wniosek Urlopowy: IPA.

Brixton Brewery: Switch: Pale ale.

Berowar Artezan: Bombelek Z Zerówki: A sour beer (I went through a phase of ordering lots of sour beers from Europe, can you tell?).

Shiny Brewery: Chill: So I need to give a shout out to the can art here. I first heard about Shiny Brewery through BBC local news. I looked them up and saw their alcohol free beer. The can is the most aesthetically pleasing thing I have seen in my entire life. It's probably the fastest I've ever checked out on a beer. The liquid itself-also very good.

Redwillow Brewery: Less Is More: A mosaic pale ale.

Chance Clean Cider: I know this is a beer book but I simply can't finish it without talking about these guys. They make the finest alcohol free cider in the country in my opinion. Everything you assumed about alcohol free cider goes out of the window when you first try this. It's absolute perfection.

And there we have it. I am certain there are beers that I have lost in my memory and there will certainly be more beers to follow, but those are, more or less, all of the alcohol-free beers I have drank since going sober in 2022. For every beer I have tried, there are ten that I haven't; that's thousands of alcohol-free beers available to be enjoyed all over the world.

This list isn't just a tally; it's a map of a journey. A journey of trial, discovery, and often delightful surprise. Each beer tells a story. Of a brewer's passion, of evolving tastes, and of a growing movement that's transforming how we think about drinking.

So whether you're a seasoned alcohol-free explorer or just dipping your toe in, remember: The shelf is vast, the options are ever-changing, and the adventure is always just a sip away (should I start a holiday company?).

8 THE FUTURE OF ALCOHOL-FREE BEER

Let's go back to 2022, sipping my first 'real' alcohol-free beer from an actual craft brewery and wondering if there could possibly be anything better than this in the entire world. The alcohol-free revolution had surely come to pass and it was not televised. Instead, it had snuck up on us. We had a handful of fairly decent beers that were now readily available. Had you asked me to think about the *future* of alcohol-free beer then, I'd have probably told you we were already there (also, I'd have probably pointed out the fact that I had no idea because I had only been drinking the stuff for a week and was very much still an alcoholic, but that's not important).

Yet here we are. The alcohol-free beer landscape is evolving faster than anybody could have predicted. What was once an ignored corner of the supermarket shelf has become a battleground of innovation and cultural change.

The future is both exciting and uncertain, a crossroads if you will. Some paths look bright and inviting, others a little foggy. What lies beyond those meandering paths depends on choices made by brewers, drinkers, retailers, and regulators.

So where is it all heading? That's a question I've heard again and again while running The Sober Boozers Club. It comes up in my DMs, at events, and on almost every podcast episode I have been a part of:

"Will alcohol-free beer keep improving?"

"Is there any point in a table beer with alcohol-free offerings at an all-time high in quality?"

"Will it still be a niche field in five years?"

"Will the bubble burst?"

The truth is, nobody can predict the future with certainty. But, based on what I have seen alongside the many conversations I've had with brewers, retailers, and fellow alcohol-free drinkers (remember, this has been my entire life for a good three years now), we can sketch out a few possibilities.

So let's do that. Not one prediction, but three: An optimistic future, a pessimistic future, and a balanced view that feels (for now) the most likely.

The Optimistic Future: A Golden Age Of Choice

Picture this, dear reader: It's a warm Friday evening at a bustling taproom. The chatter hums around you, laughter spills from a corner table and servers glide between customers with gleaming taps and glasses full of amber, gold and ruby liquid, many of them alcohol-free.

A group nearby toasts with an array of alcohol-free beers: a rich, chocolatey stout, a bright, tart Berliner weisse and a hazy IPA bursting with tropical hops. Nobody asks them why they are all drinking alcohol-free beer. No one looks askance. It's just beer. Really, really good beer. It's basically Germany right now, but we're going to go a little further because this is my beautiful new world and you can't stop me.

Alcohol-Free Beer Becomes Fully Normalised

In this future, alcohol-free beer no longer comes with an asterisk. It's simply beer. Walk into any pub or supermarket and you'll find it on tap or in the chilled aisle alongside its boozier cousins. The days of awkward glances or "glass of pop" jokes feel like a distant memory.

Retailers invest in prominent, well-organised alcohol-free sections. Pubs train staff to speak knowledgeably and enthusiastically about alcohol-free options. At festivals, alcohol-free beer flows as freely as the alcoholic kind, with tents dedicated to the stuff.

In this future, some would predict we may see an emergence of wellness bars. I, for one, don't bat for that team. I don't want to lose the classic pub experience and replace it with a sober utopia. I want alcohol-free options to become as part of drinking culture in the UK as full-alcohol beer is currently. In my future, pubs continue to be pubs, as we know them and love them. Places of laughter, warmth, debate, community and the odd wobbly stool. Only in this future, the pub will once again be something that appeals to generations who have distanced themselves from their local. A place for all, alcohol consumer or not.

The pub has always been about far more than alcohol. It's about people. Alcohol-free beer has the power to help the pub reclaim that inclusive space, where younger generations, health-conscious drinkers, the sober curious, and your everyday drinker all feel equally welcome at the bar.

In this future, landlords and brewers will have embraced this evolution; the humble pub won't have been diminished by the rise of alcohol-free beer. It will thrive.

Brewers Drive a Renaissance of Flavour

Brewers aren't playing catch-up anymore. They lead the charge with innovative, bold creations that challenge what we thought alcohol-free beer could be. Cask beer? Brewers have solved it; imperial stouts with complexity? Easy. The science of alcohol-free brewing has unlocked things we didn't ever believe possible. This could even play into the world of functional drinks. While I have stated I'm not really a believer in these beers, there is a place for them in this future, for people that do want a buzz without the booze. We could see a rise in THC and CBD beer in the UK or (this is bold) the development of a brand-new alcohol alternative that completely changes the game (I'm possibly getting carried away now).

On-Trade Transformed

Imagine walking into a restaurant where the staff eagerly recommend an alcohol-free pairing for your meal. The menu lists alcohol-free beers by style and tasting notes, just like the alcoholic ones. You can order a flight and swap stories with friends about the subtle citrus in the IPA or the toasted malt character in the brown ale. These scenes are becoming a reality in pockets of the country already, but in this future, they have become widespread.

Accessible and Affordable

Wider adoption means economies of scale. Breweries expand production lines; supermarkets dedicate more shelf space. Prices come down, making great alcohol-free beer an everyday choice rather than a treat. The 0.5% ABV myth is left to rot in the past, with worldwide adoption of the 'alcohol-free' label for all beers coming in at 0.5% or under. This comes alongside educational campaigns by industry leaders and retailers themselves, debunking the myths and misconceptions surrounding alcohol-free beer.

Culture Shift: From Stigma to Celebration

Good alcohol-free beer is available everywhere. From small to large supermarkets. Quaint country pubs to five-star hospitality venues. The cultural shift is profound. No longer viewed as a sign of weakness or sacrifice, alcohol-free beer is the new normal. Generations that have not yet been born will be shocked when they hear about the stigma that was once attached to alcohol-free beer, finding it impossible to imagine a world without it.

The Pessimistic Future: More Beer, Fewer Choices

As much as I want to live in the world above, the road ahead isn't all sunshine and roses. Let's talk about a bleaker future.

Macro Brewer Domination

Large global brewers see a massive growth opportunity in alcohol-free beer. They invest billions to flood markets with their brands, locking in supermarket shelf space and pub tap contracts.

At first glance, this means alcohol-free beer is everywhere, more visible than ever before. But there's a cost.

The market begins to resemble a monoculture. Big brands focus on mass-appeal lagers and pale ales, styles with broad but shallow flavour profiles that play it safe. Their marketing budgets outspend everyone else, drowning out the voices of small, independent brewers. The liquid itself? It stays the same. Alcohol-free beer sells just the way it is, so why change it? For most people, their first taste of alcohol-free beer will be a dull supermarket lager that is completely uninspiring. Sober-curious individuals decide to look elsewhere for their drink of choice.

The thrill of discovering a quirky, unexpected alcohol-free beer fades. Those wild sours, smoked porters, and everything in between become rare, incredibly niche gems.

Craft Breweries Squeezed

Independent alcohol-free breweries face a brutal landscape. Without the marketing muscle or distribution reach of the big players, they struggle to stay afloat. Some shift to alcoholic beer or diversify into other products. Some close their doors.

On-Trade Homogenisation

Pubs and bars, chasing profitability and deals, lean into macro-brand exclusivity. Alcohol-free taps are dominated by one or two familiar names, and craft offerings become scarce. The experience grows dull and predictable; far from the vibrant, inclusive drinking culture many had hoped for.

In this future, pubs become increasingly irrelevant to younger, health-conscious drinkers, or anybody looking to moderate. They don't feel welcome, they don't feel catered for, so they simply stop going. The pub, once a cornerstone of British social life, becomes a relic. Something older generations reminisce about while the younger lot find their community elsewhere.

While alcohol-free beer may be static in this future, the shift in people's attitude towards alcohol can't be stopped. With little to no good alcohol-free beer in venues, the traditional pub gets left behind, losing footfall and ultimately losing purpose. Not because it was pushed out by sober culture but because it refused to make room for it.

Community Frustration

People already tapped into the alcohol-free movement will see its demise in front of their own eyes. Businesses that have built their foundations on alcohol-free beverages will be hit, with consumers also suffering as the options available to them will be dramatically reduced. People who run Instagram pages dedicated to alcohol-free beer will have wasted years of their lives on a project that was always destined to be sucked up by big breweries (hi, nice to meet you).

There is also a sinister take here. For people like myself, alcohol-free beer was an essential part of my recovery. I would not be here today had it not been for alcohol-free beer. In this future, for people struggling with addiction, this potential resource would be mostly gone. This could be devastating for some in recovery.

The Balanced Prediction: Progress With Compromises

That all sounds very bleak and dramatic, doesn't it? Like you're a young child in a film that used to live with their nice parents but now you live with your nasty aunt and uncle because your parents died in a car crash kind of vibe. Don't worry though, it's just a bad dream (I hope).

This is where I think we are actually heading.

Growth Will Continue, But Unevenly

The alcohol-free beer market isn't a fad. Declining alcohol consumption across younger generations and growing health awareness will mean the demand will keep rising.

However, this growth will be patchy. Big breweries will dominate mainstream sales and visibility, while craft alcohol-free brewers remain niche but passionate.

Quality Will Continue To Improve, Slowly

Cask beer is probably off the cards for a while, but we will see gradual improvements across the board. Even macro brands are investing in better recipes. What we've seen recently with IPAs will filter into other styles, so we will get really solid stouts, bitters and (hopefully) milds. Still, a range of quality will exist, from the pedestrian to the exceptional.

Craft Will Survive Through Community

Passionate craft breweries will lean on their communities. They will have a foot in the door, which is enough to turn drinkers' heads in their direction. Once people have sampled one exceptional craft beer from an independent brewery, they will keep coming back for more. There will be a rise of commentators both in physical and digital form, discussing the ever-growing range of options that will fuel the craft alcohol-free movement.

On-Trade Improvement Will Be Patchy

We will still see the big hitters in most bars: Guinness, Heineken, Becks Blue, Erdinger, Stella. Some pubs will embrace alcohol-free beer wholeheartedly, others will lag behind. The pubs that embrace the change will start offering a well-curated range of alcohol-free beer in addition to (or instead of) the big names listed above. They will understand that adding a good alcohol-free line-up does not replace the pub experience, it enhances it. The pubs lagging behind? They will stick to those known brands and ultimately suffer for it.

Overall? I think the pub will survive. It will adapt, as it has many times before. From smoking bans to the craft beer revolution to contactless payments, pubs have evolved with the times. Alcohol-free beer is just another chapter in that story.

Culture Will Keep Evolving

Choosing alcohol-free beer will become increasingly normal and accepted. This cultural change, although the most simple, may be the most important factor shaping the future. More so than any marketing campaign or high-profile release.

Final Thoughts

The future of alcohol-free beer is a story still being written. By brewers, drinkers, retailers, and venues.

If we want the optimistic future, a golden age of quality, diversity, and celebration, we'll need to back it up with our choices. Buy the beers you love, ask for better options, and support smaller brewers. Celebrate big breweries when they get it right and hold them accountable when they don't.

As we stand on the brink of what could be the era of alcohol-free beer, it's worth remembering the community we have built together. Every bottle opened, every pint poured, every shared recommendation adds a drop to this growing tide. The journey from those early, often disappointing alcohol-free beers to the vibrant, diverse scene we see today has been remarkable. As for the road ahead? It's full of promise, challenge, and opportunity. I have seen the growth in this sector over the past few years with my own eyes. As I look ahead, I'm hopeful. I believe the best days of alcohol-free beer are still ahead of us.

CONCLUSION

Here we are. If you've made it this far, thank you. I hope you have found something useful, something surprising, and maybe even a few beers to hunt down within these pages.

When I first gave up alcohol, I could not have dreamed it would lead me here. I thought it would be a quiet personal choice, not something that would become a passion, a platform, and now a book. I certainly didn't expect to be several hundred beers deep, swapping notes with brewers and running a community with thousands of fellow alcohol-free beer lovers along for the ride. Life has a way of surprising you when you give it the space.

If there's one thing I've learned on this journey, it's this: Alcohol-free beer is not about removing something. It's the opposite. It's about broadening the landscape of how we drink, socialise, and celebrate. It's about saying, "You can still have that pint in hand, it just doesn't have to cost you tomorrow."

That shift in mindset is powerful. It's helping reshape the conversation around sobriety, moderation, and drinking culture as a whole, one pint, can, bottle at a time.

Now, I'm under no illusions. Not everyone will embrace this change. There will always be sceptics who take the mick. But for every one of them, there's someone discovering a new alcohol-free beer they love. Someone having a great night out and waking up fresh the next morning. Someone who realises that pubs and pints don't have to go hand-in-hand with alcohol consumption if you don't want them to.

That is why I wrote this book. Not to say that everyone should stop drinking alcohol. Not to pretend that alcohol-free beer is perfect (it isn't, yet). But to show that there is another way. A way that lets beer lovers like me (and maybe like you) stay connected to the rituals, the flavours, and the culture of beer, without sacrificing wellbeing.

The future of alcohol-free beer is bright. The choice is growing. The quality is improving, and the more we show up and demand great alcohol-free options, be it in pubs, bars, bottle shops, or at festivals, the more the industry will respond.

So, whether you're reading this as a committed alcohol-free convert, a curious explorer, or just someone curious about the good alternatives on a night out, I hope this book has helped you to feel part of something bigger. Because that's what it is, a movement built from the ground up, by people who believe that choice is worth celebrating.

Talking about alcohol-free beer has been the honour of my life. It has taken me to places I could have never imagined, opened doors I believed were set to be shut forever. I rediscovered myself through alcohol-free beer, I reclaimed my life with alcohol-free beer. I'll keep drinking, reviewing, rambling, and defending alcohol-free beer for the rest of my life. The list of beers will continue to grow (they'll probably outgrow me). The community will keep expanding, and hopefully, more pubs, breweries, and drinkers will join us along the way.

So here's to alcohol-free beer. The people who make it, drink it, champion it. We've come a long way, but the best is yet to come.

Cheers!

ABOUT THE AUTHOR

Ben Gibbs has been a beer commentator and sobriety awareness activist since he gave up alcohol in January 2022. Having sampled over 700 alcohol-free beers from across the globe, Ben has worked alongside multiple breweries, appeared regularly on radio, given talks at beer festivals and became the first alcoholic in active recovery to win a British Guild Of Beer Writers award for communication about beer. He was also invited to Parliament to meet with ministers in January 2025 on behalf of Alcohol Change UK. An ever-present face in the world of alcohol-free beer, Ben became the first alcohol-free beer commentator to release a collaboration beer with UK Indie brewery We Can Be Friends. Ben is passionate about alcohol-free beer, having claimed the liquid saved his life, and has dedicated his life to helping others discover its potential, whether on a sober journey or not.

Printed in Dunstable, United Kingdom